Relish

NORTH EAST & YORKSHIRE

SECOND HELPING

Original recipes from the North East
and Yorkshire's finest chefs and
restaurants. Introduction by celebrity chefs
James Martin and Hairy Biker, Si King.

First Published 2013
By Relish Publications
Shield Green Farm, Tritlington,
Northumberland, NE61 3DX.

ISBN: 978-0-9575370-2-6

Publisher: Duncan L Peters
General Manager: Teresa Peters
Design: Vicki Brown
Relish Photography: Tim Green, Kevin Gibson,
Nicky Rogerson and Adrian Gatie
Editorial Consultant: Paul Robertson
Editorial Assistant: Gillian Scribbins
Special thanks to Erin Salati

Front cover photograph by Tim Green

Printed By: Balto Print Ltd, Stratford,
London E15 2TF.

Relish
PUBLICATIONS

Relish
OUR HAND PICKED RESTAURANTS

As the proud owner of a Relish cookbook, you may subscribe for your own personal Relish Rewards card which entitles you to free membership for one year.

You can access the Relish members' area on our website and find out what exclusive offers are available to you from the fantastic restaurants featured in our series of books throughout the UK. Look out for the Relish Rewards card icon at the end of each restaurant's introduction.

TO RECEIVE YOUR CARD
Simply register on our homepage www.relishpublications.co.uk or email relishrewards@relishpublications.co.uk and we will post your exclusive Relish Rewards card.

When you book, just let the restaurant know that you are a member and take your card along with you.

WHAT ARE THE REWARDS?
The rewards will continue to be updated on the website so do check and keep in touch. These range from a free bottle of Champagne to free gifts when you dine. Relish will send you a quarterly newsletter with special discounts, rewards and free recipes, We are about quality not quantity!

All offers are subject to change. See the Relish website for details.

www.relishpublications.co.uk

004
CONTENTS

DESSERTS

006
CONTENTS

DESMNTS DESSERTS

RESTAURANTS

008
CONTENTS

DESSERTS

RESTAURANTS

INTRODUCTION TO YORKSHIRE WITH JAMES MARTIN

Delivering tasty, good food is all about working with quality produce, drawing out those delicious flavours and marrying them with other tastes and textures to complement one another. My suppliers are the best and I speak with them all the time. I urge home cooks to talk to their butcher, greengrocer, game supplier and fishmonger. Use what's in season, engage with them and you will be rewarded. We are so fortunate in Yorkshire with our thriving independent traders, vibrant food markets and a booming number of artisan food producers and we must champion them.

And eat out. Choose independently run restaurants and pubs where chefs work tirelessly to provide us with outstanding, imaginative cooking coupled with great service. Be adventurous and enjoy dishes you may not prepare at home. Yorkshire is a great place to discover new and exciting food as well as the best classical cooking in the country.

Happy eating.

Y orkshire! The county that has it all; more than its fair share of quality restaurants and pubs and more Michelin stars than any other county outside of London. Plus, Yorkshire has an abundance of seriously good food producers delivering to our kitchens the best from land and water.

It gives me enormous pleasure every time I return to my home town of Malton, which in recent years has become known as a town for foodies with its food lovers' markets and festivals. It's here that I have my own restaurant at the Talbot Hotel. I enjoy nothing more than getting back into the kitchen to work with the chefs there, creating new and exciting seasonal dishes utilising the food from the local area.

James Martin
The Talbot Hotel

INTRODUCTION TO THE NORTH EAST WITH SI KING

'm proud to live in the North!

I'm particularly proud of the producers who work tirelessly to bring the great yield of our region to our attention and our plates. This book would simply not be possible without them. Our chefs need great produce to work with and good chefs let the quality of ingredients speak for themselves.

It is not a new concept that we are all products of our environment, our produce especially is defined by the topography of our great British regions. It has always been my opinion that buying seasonally and locally, where possible, is the best way to shop, as one is in receipt of the best the locale has to offer at the peak of its quality.

The most important action of any food producer is to endeavour to bring new people to the party. Widening a marketplace is a challenge - you must react to the different needs of people's tastes and pockets, but we're Northerners! And we've never shied away from a challenge.

The future for our regional food is bright, exciting times lay ahead. Celebrate, educate, discuss and inform. Support our producers; it's going to become even more important given the economic climate. Dave and I look forward to exploring it as individuals and together as the Hairy Bikers.

I'll leave you with this thought. It's a quote from chef de patron, Terry Laybourne;

"90% of good cooking is good shopping."

Enjoy the book. I have!

Love to all

Si King, Hairy Bikers

012
No 59 OLD ELVET

The Durham Marriott Hotel Royal County, 59 Old Elvet, Durham, DH1 3JN

0191 386 6821 (extension 437)
www.DurhamMarriottRoyalCounty.co.uk

No 59 Old Elvet is located at... No 59 Old Elvet, on the ground floor of the Durham Marriott Hotel Royal County. This iconic, four star property is an amalgam of several buildings, the oldest of which dates from circa 1630. A trade directory from 1890 lists No 59 Old Elvet as Plews & Sons - wine and spirit merchants - providing the inspiration for our 'Plews Pudding' recipe. The restaurant was formerly known as the County Restaurant and has been recently renamed as part of the hotel's 'back to the future' repositioning, which emphasises the unique history of the site and highlights a proud tradition of hospitality and service that stretches back almost 200 years.

This recently refurbished restaurant exudes warmth and charm through the use of rich, vibrant, tasteful colours, whilst high-backed leather chairs and Wenge-stained oak flooring emphasise the restaurant's classical roots. Artwork adorning the walls and bold blue milk glass give the restaurant a contemporary edge. In the evening, overhead lighting is dimmed and table lanterns are lit to add warmth and to create an intimate atmosphere.

Head chef James Marron and his team have created a menu that features steaks and seafood and includes signature dishes like those highlighted on the following pages. Our beverage selection includes a range of classic and contemporary Martinis, which are shaken and poured at tableside; 30 white, red, rosé and sparkling wines, with 11 served by the glass; Black Sheep Bitter on draft and premium spirits such as Grey Goose vodka.

The tableside interaction between servers and customers is one of the qualities that set us apart from other restaurants.

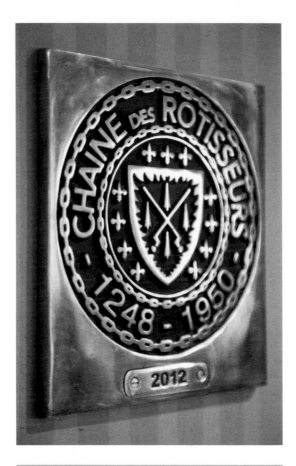

Relish Restaurant Rewards
See page 003 for details.

Service manager Ruth Paisley and her team have an in-depth understanding of all the dishes they serve, including their historical roots, and tailor their approach to each table.

Menu descriptions are brief, as our service team are always pleased to share their recommendations and extensive knowledge of the menu. The service style reflects a certain classic elegance and uses traditional values without being old fashioned.

Accessed via the main hotel entrance or directly from Old Elvet, No 59 Old Elvet is open daily for dinner from 6.30pm.

HOT CRASTER SMOKIES, SOURDOUGH CHARDS

SERVES 1

🍷 *Robert Mondavi Twin Oaks Chardonnay, 2011/12*
(California, USA)

Ingredients

100g natural smoked haddock fillet
75ml double cream
15g strong Cheddar (grated)
15g Parmesan (grated)
10g breadcrumbs
salt and pepper (pinch of)

75g sourdough baguette

Method

For The Smokies

Cut the smoked haddock fillet into four even sized pieces.

Place the smoked haddock pieces in an earthenware dish and layer with the Cheddar and Parmesan cheese.

Season the cream with salt and pepper.

Cover the smoked haddock with the seasoned cream.

Place in an oven preheated to 175°C and cook for ten to 12 minutes.

Remove the dish from the oven.

Sprinkle with breadcrumbs (see chef's tip) and place under the grill until the breadcrumbs turn golden in colour.

Chef's Tip

Grate the two ends of the sourdough baguette and use the breadcrumbs to create a more rustic texture.

For The Sourdough Bread Chards

Slice the sourdough baguette thinly (approximately 10mm in width) on a 45° angle. Place under a grill and toast until golden on both sides.

To Serve

Place the earthenware dish on a plate or wooden board and build a stack of the sourdough chards to one side.

LAMB RUMP, CARAMELISED SHALLOTS, WENSLEYDALE BLUE CAULIFLOWER CHEESE & CLARET JUS

SERVES 1

🍷 *Chateau Lamothe-Cissac, Cru Bourgeois*
Haut-Medoc, 2006/7 (France)

Ingredients

Lamb
225g Nidderdale lamb rump
salt and pepper (pinch of)

Wensleydale Blue Cauliflower Cheese
75g cauliflower florets (*blanched*)
50ml béchamel sauce (warmed)
50g Wensleydale blue cheese (crumbled)
25g breadcrumbs

Shallots
2 banana shallots (peeled)
5ml olive oil
salt and pepper (pinch of)

Claret Jus
25g shallots (finely diced)
50ml Claret
15g unsalted butter
50ml beef or veal jus
salt and pepper (to taste)

Method

Remove the lamb rump from the fridge about 30 minutes before cooking to allow it to come back to room temperature.

For The Cauliflower Cheese

Arrange the *blanched* cauliflower florets in an earthenware dish. Evenly pour over the warm béchamel sauce and sprinkle over the Wensleydale blue cheese. Bake in an oven, preheated to 180°C, for 20 minutes. Remove the cauliflower cheese from the oven, sprinkle with breadcrumbs and place under the grill until the breadcrumbs turn golden in colour.

For The Shallots

Drizzle olive oil over the banana shallots and season with salt and pepper. Roast in an oven preheated to 180°C for around seven to ten minutes or until soft, tender and golden.

> **Chef's Tip**
>
> *Blanch* the banana shallots in salted boiling water for five minutes and then put straight into cold water until required. This will ensure the shallots are softer in the middle and will caramelise all the way through during roasting.

For The Lamb Rump

Baste the lamb rump in a little olive oil and season with salt and pepper. Add a little olive oil to a frying pan and sauté over a moderate heat until cooked to your liking (for pink 15 to 20 minutes, for well-done 25 to 30 minutes). Retain the oil in the pan. Remove the lamb from the pan and allow to rest for five minutes before carving.

For The Claret Jus

Add the butter and finely diced shallots to the pan used to fry the lamb rump and cook until soft and translucent. Then add the Claret and simmer until the amount of liquid is reduced by half. Add the beef or veal jus and reduce a little more, then remove from the heat. Season with salt and pepper to taste.

To Serve

Stack the shallots on the plate. Carve the lamb rump on a 45° angle. Place the lamb rump on the plate next to the shallots and dress with the Claret jus. Serve with the cauliflower cheese.

PLEWS PUDDING*
BLACK SHEEP ALE BREAD & BUTTER PUDDING WITH CREME ANGLAISE

*59 Old Elvet was listed in Kellys Trade Directory of 1890 as Plews & Sons wine and spirit merchants

SERVES 4

Marsala Wine
(Sicily)

Ingredients

Bread And Butter Pudding

50g sultanas
50ml Black Sheep Ale
25g unsalted butter, plus a little extra for greasing
8 slices brown bread
brown sugar (for sprinkling)

Ale Syrup

250ml Black Sheep Ale
25g brown sugar

Custard

350ml double cream
4 whole eggs
2 egg yolks
$1/4$ tsp nutmeg
$1/4$ tsp cinnamon
50g brown sugar

Crème Anglaise

6 egg yolks
65g caster sugar
2 vanilla pods (split lengthwise, seeds scraped out and pod chopped)
500ml full fat milk

4 ramekins (7cm diameter)

Chef's Tip

Do not add sultanas to the top layer of the pudding as they will burn during cooking.

Method

For The Ale Syrup

Pour the Black Sheep Ale and brown sugar into a heavy bottomed saucepan and simmer until the amount of liquid reduces by half. Remove from the stove and allow to cool for use later.

For The Crème Anglaise

In a heavy bottomed saucepan, bring the milk, with the chopped vanilla pods and seeds, to a boil and simmer for five to six minutes. Allow this to cool for two to three minutes.

Place the egg yolks and sugar in a large mixing bowl and cream until pale and fluffy. Gently add the milk to the egg and sugar mixture a little at a time, whisking continuously, until smooth and creamy. Pour the mixture back into the heavy bottomed saucepan and return to a gentle heat. Continue to stir until the mixture has thickened enough to coat the back of a spoon. Strain the mixture through a fine sieve and serve in a jug, or alternatively refrigerate until required.

For The Bread And Butter Pudding

Soak the sultanas in the Black Sheep Ale until they become plump. Grease four ramekins (approximately 7cm diameter) with the extra butter. Cut the crusts off the bread, spread each slice with butter and cut each slice into four small triangles.

Arrange a layer of bread in the bottom of the ramekins and sprinkle with the soaked sultanas and brown sugar. Repeat the layers of bread, sultanas and sugar until you have used up all the bread. Finish with a layer of bread and sugar.

For The Custard (To soak in the pudding)

Gently warm the cream in a pan until it reaches scalding point, taking care not to let it boil. Whisk the eggs, egg yolk, cinnamon, nutmeg and the brown sugar in a bowl until pale.

Add the Black Sheep ale syrup (prepared earlier) to the warm cream mixture and stir well. Add this to the egg mix. Strain and pour over the prepared bread layers. Sprinkle with a little more brown sugar. Leave to stand for 30 to 35 minutes to allow the custard to soak in. Preheat the oven to 160°C. Place the ramekins into the oven and bake for 20 to 25 minutes or until the custard has set and the top is golden in colour.

To Serve

Serve in the ramekins (or if you really want to impress, in small copper saucepans) and serve with the Crème Anglaise.

022
THE BAY HORSE HURWORTH

45 The Green, Hurworth, Darlington, County Durham, DL2 2AA

01325 720 663
www.thebayhorsehurworth.com

The Bay Horse at Hurworth serves exceptional, award-winning, gastro-pub style food. It is a firm favourite among locals and visitors alike, and diners travel many miles to enjoy what the restaurant has to offer.

The menu we serve is made up of top quality, classic English dishes with a twist. Locally sourced produce is used wherever possible by the chefs to make the most of seasonal produce and all bread is baked on site with a different selection every day. There's also a Prix Fixe lunch, which changes every day and includes a traditional Sunday lunch.

Located in the exclusive village of Hurworth, on the outskirts of Darlington, the Bay Horse is jointly owned by experienced restaurateurs Marcus Bennett and Jonathan Hall. The building dates back to the 1400s and underwent an extensive refurbishment in 2008 when Marcus and Jonathan took over the pub.

Marcus works very closely with his team of chefs to create modernised pub classics such as belly pork, braised beef and caramelised rice pudding.

The emphasis is on the finer details of a real English pub - dimpled pint glasses, side dishes served in copper pans, an open fire in the main bar and hand pulled local ales. All furnishings were carefully sourced from antique fairs around the country, including two late Victorian dining tables in the private dining rooms upstairs.

 Relish Restaurant Rewards
See page 003 for details.

The Bay Horse at Hurworth is no stranger to awards and recognition. In addition to The Bay Horse winning a Michelin Bib Gourmand for the last four years, Gastro Pub Chef of the Year for Marcus and being listed in the top ten for the Gastro Pub awards, they were also listed in Sawday Pubs & Inns and featured as an Inspectors' Favourite in the Michelin Eating out in Pubs Guide 2011 and 2012. They also feature in the Michelin Restaurant Guide 2012 and the Good Food Guide and have had write-ups in local and national papers, including the Sunday Times.

POTTED CRAB, BEETROOT MOUSSE & BEETROOT PURÉE

SERVES 4

🍷 *Unwooded Chardonnay 2011 Rustenberg Stellenbosch (South Africa)*

Ingredients

Potted Crab

200g white crabmeat
2 egg yolks
1 tsp Dijon mustard
2 tsp white wine vinegar
5ml lemon juice
2 tsp dry sherry
2 tsp Worcestershire sauce
2g cayenne pepper
1g grated nutmeg
salt (pinch of)
200ml grapeseed oil
50ml olive oil
1 banana shallot (finely diced)
100g chives (finely chopped)

Beetroot Purée

200g raw beetroot (grated)
100ml apple juice
35ml white wine vinegar
65ml port

Beetroot Mousse

25g cooked beetroot (finely diced)
50g beetroot purée
$3/4$ gelatine leaf (soaked in cold water)
25g crispy pancetta (chopped and cooked)
1 shallot (finely diced)
100ml double cream (semi-whipped)

Garnish

mixed leaves
25g cooked beetroot (cubed and pickled in vinegar)
beetroot relish (we make our own but can be shop bought)
chervil
1 piece of toast (cut into soldiers)

4 glass jars

Method

For The Purée

Place the beetroot in a pan with the port, apple juice and white wine vinegar. Cook over a low heat for one hour until almost all the liquid has evaporated. Blend to a purée and pass through a fine sieve.

For The Mousse

Add the soaked gelatine to 50g of the beetroot purée and blend. Pass through a fine sieve into a bowl, then chill. Stir from time to time and, when nearly set, add the semi-whipped cream, diced beetroot, shallots and pancetta. Pipe the beetroot mousse into the glass jars and half fill them. Leave to set for one hour.

For The Crab

Place the egg yolks, Dijon mustard, salt, sherry, white wine vinegar, Worcestershire sauce, nutmeg, cayenne pepper and lemon juice in an electric mixer and whisk until pale and fluffy. Mix the two oils together and slowly add to the egg mix in a thin trickle, whisking all the time. Finally, fold in the shallots, chives, and white crabmeat.

To Assemble And Serve

Top the mousse with the white crabmeat and mixed leaves. Swipe the remaining beetroot purée on a plate and place the jar just off the middle. Garnish with chervil, cubed pickled beetroot and a *quenelle* of beetroot relish. Place a toasted soldier in the crab pot.

> **Chef's Tip**
> Make sure the mousse is set before placing the crab on top.

BRAISED BEEF WITH DUCK FAT CARROTS, CARROT PUREE, RED WINE JUS & BABY SUET PUDDING

SERVES 4

🍷 *Château la Tour de Mons 2007 Margaux, Bordeaux (France)*

Ingredients

4 x small moulds for suet pudding

Braised Beef

4 x 500g beef cheeks (trimmed of all fat)
2 cloves garlic (whole)
1 stick celery (chopped), 1 onion (chopped)
1 bay leaf, 1 sprig thyme
250ml red wine, 1ltr chicken stock
1 tsp salt, $^1/_2$ tsp white pepper
knob of butter

Carrot Purée

300g carrots (peeled and chopped)
25g unsalted butter
200ml jelly chicken stock
100ml double cream
4g caster sugar, 2 lemons (juice of)

Suet Crust Pastry

110g self-raising flour
75ml cold water (to mix)
55g shredded suet
$^1/_2$ tsp salt

Beef Suet Pudding

200g beef cheek (cooked and diced)
100ml red wine
1 carrot (diced into $^1/_2$" pieces)
5 button mushrooms (diced)
2 rashers bacon (cooked and finely diced)
1 tsp thyme (chopped), 1 tsp parsley (chopped)
$^1/_2$ clove garlic (crushed)
100ml veal stock
2 tsp English mustard powder
5g plain flour, $^1/_2$ tbsp salt

4 finger carrots
2 tbsp duck fat
spinach (cooked), chervil (to garnish)

Method

For The Beef (Prepare the day before)

Marinate the trimmed beef cheeks overnight in the wine, garlic and vegetables. In a hot frying pan, add a little oil and brown the cheeks of beef on all sides. Remove from the pan and sprinkle with salt and pepper. Place in a deep baking tray and pour in the vegetables and wine marinade. Add the herbs and the chicken stock. Finally, lay a piece of greaseproof paper directly on top of the wine mixture and cover the tray with tinfoil. Bake at 150°C for six hours. Remove from the oven and leave to rest in the liquid in the fridge until cold. Remove the beef from the stock and cut into 150g square portions. Bring the sauce to a boil, reduce by two thirds and pass through a fine sieve.

For The Carrots

Place the carrots in a pan with the butter and cover with a lid. Cook for ten minutes. Add the chicken stock, caster sugar and lemon and cook until the carrots are very soft, approximately one hour. Add the cream and blend to a fine purée.

For The Pastry

Sieve the flour and salt into a large bowl. Add the suet and mix lightly. Mix with sufficient water to make soft, but firm dough. Turn out on to a lightly floured work surface. Knead gently until smooth.

For The Beef Suet Pudding

Cook the bacon, button mushrooms, garlic and carrot in a little oil. Stir in the flour and mustard powder, then pour in the red wine and veal stock. Bring to a boil and simmer for 20 minutes. Add the beef cheeks, leave to cool and finally add the parsley and thyme. Roll out the suet pastry and line a small mould with it. Press the beef mix into it and top with suet pastry. Steam in a steamer for 45 minutes (you can place in a Chinese steamer over a pan of simmering water).

To Serve

Preheat the oven to 180°C and cook the suet pudding for ten minutes. Place the braised beef portions in a small dish and cover with the sauce and a small knob of butter. Return to the oven and cook for five minutes. Peel the finger carrots and slice in half. Place in a pan with salted boiling water and cook until soft. Heat the duck fat in a pan and place the carrots in face down and cook until brown. On a large plate place the beef on a small mound of spinach and put the suet pudding to one side. Swipe the carrot purée and place the carrots on top of the beef and suet pudding. Finally, drizzle with a little of the beef sauce. Garnish with chervil.

RICE PUDDING WITH BRAMBLE JAM & BLACKBERRY ICE CREAM

SERVES 4

🍷 *Mitchell Noble Semillon 2010 , Clare Valley (Australia)*

Ingredients

Rice Pudding

80g Arborio rice
125ml full fat milk
1/2 vanilla pod (seeds scraped out)
1/2 tsp vanilla extract
10ml brandy
30g clotted cream
30g condensed milk
75ml double cream
demerara sugar (for glazing)

Blackberry Purée

250g frozen blackberries
100g sugar

Bramble Jam

2kg blackberries
1kg caster sugar
2 lemons (juice and zest of)
85ml water

Ice Cream

200ml cream
300ml milk
5 egg yolks
75g sugar
1 tbsp glucose
15g butter

Method

For The Rice Pudding

Mix the rice with the vanilla seeds, vanilla extract, brandy, clotted cream and condensed milk and place in a gastro pan. Cover the rice with greaseproof paper and cover the gastro pan with tinfoil. Bake in a preheated oven for 40 minutes at 170°C. Remove from the oven.

For The Bramble Jam

Wash, then place the blackberries, lemon and water into a large, deep, heavy bottomed pan and stew over a gentle heat for 20 minutes or until the fruit is soft. Remove from heat and use a hand blender to blend. Return to a gentle heat and slowly stir in all the sugar until it has dissolved. Turn up the heat to high and bring to a hard boil for eight minutes or until the jam has reached setting point. To find out the setting point, simply spoon a little jam onto a cold plate and put in the fridge for a minute, then push the jam with a spoon. If it does not immediately run back to its original position you have reached a set. Pass through a sieve and store.

For The Blackberry Purée

Place the blackberries in a pan with the sugar, cover with a lid and cook until soft. Remove the lid and cook until almost all the liquid has evaporated. Blend to a purée and pass through a fine sieve.

For The Ice Cream

Bring the milk and cream to the boil in a pan with the butter. Whisk in the glucose. Whisk the egg yolks with the sugar until pale and creamy. Pour the milk and cream over the egg and sugar mixture and whisk over a low heat until the mixture reaches 82°C, whisking all the time. Pass through a fine sieve and then fold in the blackberry purée.

Place the ice cream in an ice cream machine and churn until it is almost firm, then place in the freezer.

To Serve

Put the rice pudding in a pan with the 75ml of cream and warm through. Divide the rice pudding between four copper pans or pots. Sprinkle the tops with demerara sugar and glaze with a blow torch. Sprinkle more demerara sugar on top and glaze again. Put the bramble jam in a small killer jar with a teaspoon in, ball the ice cream and place on top of the rice pudding.

Chef's Tip

Always keep the blow torch a little away from the sugar when glazing for a golden brown finish and double glaze for extra crispness.

032
BISTRO 21

Aykley Heads House, Aykley Heads, Durham City, DH1 5AN

0191 384 4354
www.bistrotwentyone.co.uk

With its rustic-chic charm, white-washed walls and pitch pine floors, Bistro 21 is a beautiful restaurant just outside Durham city centre. It has the hum of contentment and comfort borne from the perfect lunch or satisfying supper.

It's about pared down elegance in both food and surroundings. Painted brickwork and rustic furniture hint at the simple things in life. Bistro-style dishes are served in simple, warm surroundings. You can relax in a comfortable and informal setting and easily lose a few hours in good company.

We provide classic, flavoursome food with fuss-free presentation; you provide the good company.

For those balmy, summer days, there's a cosy, sun-trap courtyard where you can hear the birds in nearby trees while eating al fresco. This flagged courtyard is ideal for private reception drinks, where musicians can play in the covered 'cloisters'.

The quirky nature of our old building means we have lots of different rooms that are ideal for special parties, groups or meetings. With a separate entrance, private bar and dedicated team of waiters, our upstairs room offers a unique private dining experience.

Bistro 21 is also the perfect, quirky location for that personal-style wedding or civil partnership. If your ceremony is at Durham Registry Office, we're right next door and can provide a reception with a truly individual spin.

Whether it's a breezy lunch, afternoon tea, buffet supper or smart dinner, we're small and flexible enough to accommodate your needs.

 Relish Restaurant Rewards
See page 003 for details.

Food without cliché, just the good stuff. Bistro-style dishes served in simple surroundings with just the right amount of chic.

CRAB SALAD

SERVES 4

🍷 *A dry German Riesling is ideal, in this case the Villa Wolf from Pfalz. Some may like to try a Vinho Verde from Portugal.*

Method

For The Crab

Pick carefully through the white crabmeat to remove any fragments of shell. Chill until needed. Pass the brown crabmeat through a fine sieve, then combine with the mayonnaise and chill. When ready to serve, combine the white crabmeat and brown crab mayonnaise with the coriander, chilli and lime juice. Check the seasoning and adjust if necessary. Spoon the crabmeat into a 65mm ring mould and gently smooth the top.

To Serve

Toss the salad leaves, apple, radishes and chives with the olive oil and lemon juice. Arrange the salad on top of the crab and serve sourdough toast alongside.

Chef's Tip

If possible, buy a large cock crab for this salad and extract the meat yourself. It always seems to taste better that way and, of course, guarantees freshness.

Ingredients

Crab

300g freshly picked white crabmeat
80g fresh brown crabmeat
1 tbsp mayonnaise
1 tbsp coriander (chopped)
1 red chilli (deseeded and finely chopped)
$^{1}/_{2}$ lime (juice of)

Salad

1 handful salad leaves
chopped chives (pinch of)
1 Granny Smith apple (cut into 2mm batons)
2 radishes (finely sliced)
1 tbsp extra virgin olive oil
$^{1}/_{2}$ lemon (juice of)
sourdough bread (toasted)

4 x 65mm ring moulds

FILLET STEAK AU POIVRE

SERVES 4

🍷 *Something relatively big from the Rhone such as a Côtes du Ventoux from Delas or, if you really want to push the boat out, Châteauneuf-du-Pape, Domaine Caillou or a Gigondas, Château du Trignon.*

Ingredients

Steak

4 x 170g fillet steaks
3 tbsp black peppercorns
3 tbsp white peppercorns
2 tbsp coriander seeds
1$^{1}/_{2}$ tsp fine sea salt
2 tbsp vegetable oil
2 tbsp soft butter

Sauce

75ml Cognac
200ml brown chicken stock
180ml double cream
3 tbsp soft green peppercorns (in brine)

To Serve

crispy chips and green beans (to serve)

Method

For The Steak

Coarsely grind the black and white peppercorns together with the coriander seeds, using a spice grinder or a pestle and mortar. Transfer the crushed peppercorns to a sieve and shake to release and discard any pepper dust. Roll the steaks in the crushed pepper, pressing firmly to embed them into the meat. Set aside at room temperature. Heat a large, heavy cast iron frying pan over a high heat and add the vegetable oil. Season the steaks with salt and place carefully into the frying pan. It is vital that the pan is very hot at this stage as the addition of the cold steaks will cool the pan, resulting in the meat stewing rather than frying. Cook for two minutes over a high heat, then add the butter. Continue cooking until the blood rises to the surface. Turn the meat over at this point. Cook for a further two minutes for rare; four minutes for medium rare; or continue until the blood rises again to the surface for medium. When cooked to your liking, remove from the pan. Transfer to a plate with a smaller, upturned plate on top (to help collect any juices which may be released whilst resting). Leave to rest in a warm place, above the stove or on the open door of a low oven.

> **Chef's Tip**
> Remove the steaks from the fridge half an hour before you cook them in order for the meat to come to room temperature.

For The Sauce

Discard any excess fat from the frying pan and swill out with the Cognac. Return to the heat and boil until reduced to one teaspoon before adding the chicken stock. Boil until reduced by three quarters, then pour in the cream. Simmer gently until reduced to a coating consistency. Strain through a fine sieve into another small saucepan. Stir in the soft green peppercorns. Check the sauce for seasoning and set aside to keep warm.

To Serve

Transfer the steaks to warm serving plates. Tip any collected juice into the sauce and spoon over the meat. Serve with thin, crispy chips, green beans or a green salad dressed in olive oil, best quality red wine vinegar and a little Dijon mustard.

RASPBERRY SOUFFLE

SERVES 4

🍷 *The ideal accompaniment would be a glass of Barsac which, unfortunately, is often hard to find. A fairly rich Monbazillac from Château Belingard is a worthy replacement to help emphasise the clean flavours of the soufflé.*

Method

For The Crumble

Place the flour and sugar in a bowl and mix well. Rub the butter into the flour mixture. Keep rubbing until the mixture resembles breadcrumbs.

For The Soufflé

Brush four soufflé moulds liberally with softened butter and coat with 20g of caster sugar. Chill in the refrigerator. Reserve eight of the raspberries in a small dish and pour over half of the vodka - leave to macerate. Liquidise the remaining raspberries with 40g of the caster sugar until smooth. Strain through a fine sieve into a small saucepan and warm over a gentle heat. Mix the remaining alcohol into the potato starch to form a smooth paste and pour into the hot raspberry purée. Whisk until thick. Remove from heat.

Whisk the egg whites in a large bowl until they form soft peaks. Shower in the remaining 210g caster sugar and continue whisking until stiff. Beat a third of the whipped egg whites into the raspberry mixture, then very gently fold in the rest.

Fill the prepared moulds with the mixture, to three quarters of the depth of the moulds. Place two of the macerated raspberries in the centre of each. Fill with more soufflé mixture to the brim and level the tops using a palette knife. Run the point of a small paring knife around the rim of the mould to ease the mixture away from the edge. Scatter each soufflé with one tablespoon of crumble. Bake at 180°C for approximately eight minutes until risen. Remove the soufflés from the oven and dust the surface with icing sugar. Serve immediately with raspberry ripple ice cream.

Chef's Tip

There's really nothing to fear from this soufflé. Follow the instructions carefully, use a fan oven and impress yourself!

Ingredients

4 tbsp unsalted butter (softened)
270g caster sugar
240g raspberries
10g potato starch
4 tsp vodka
360g egg whites
icing sugar (for dusting)

Crumble

50g granulated sugar
50g soft butter (cubed at room temperature)
80g plain flour

To Serve

raspberry ripple ice cream

THE BLUE BICYCLE

34 Fossgate, York, YO1 9TA

01904 673 990
www.thebluebicycle.com

ased in the centre of York, The Blue Bicycle is one of the city's most talked about restaurants, where we serve award-winning food in a relaxed dining atmosphere. We are highly commended for our fresh fish dishes, homemade desserts and our extensive selection of fine wines.

At the turn of the last century, our cellar was a brothel of some repute. In fact, if you wander downstairs, you will see photographs of some of the girls who, perhaps, plied their wares. We now serve romantic dinners in the private vaulted booths (or beds), which are situated in the opulent and atmospheric dining area. You can enjoy a pre-dinner tipple overlooking the river Foss, reflecting on this bygone era of impropriety.

The upstairs dining area exudes warmth and a busy atmosphere, with an eclectic range of tables and chairs, all beautifully presented. Lunch or dinner with us is a high quality dining experience in exemplary surroundings, set in an intriguingly historic building - even by York's standards. We are totally committed to your comfort and relaxation and we pride ourselves on courteous attention to detail, a friendly approach and flexibility of service. We use the freshest ingredients, prepared and presented to the highest standards.

Situated alongside the River Foss we also offer beautiful modern rooms. The Blue Rooms are luxurious, convenient, private and comfortable - perfect for leisure or business visitors or short romantic breaks. The rooms have a cool, minimalist feel with tasteful, contemporary interiors.

Our wish is to ensure that your time spent with us is truly enjoyable, and memorable, whether it is for a meal in our restaurant or a stay in the Blue Rooms. Please see our website www.thebluebicycle.com for further details.

Relish Restaurant Rewards
See page 003 for details.

Based in the centre of York, The Blue Bicycle is one of the city's most talked about restaurants, where we serve award-winning food in a relaxed dining atmosphere.

GIN & TONIC CURED SALMON, FRISEE LETTUCE, CORAL MAYONNAISE, SQUID TOAST

SERVES 4

🍷 *Hidden Bay Sauvignon*
(New Zealand)

Ingredients

Salmon

400g fresh salmon (bones removed and washed)
100g salt
100g sugar
1 tbsp juniper berries (crushed)
3 limes (juice and zest)
25ml gin
125ml Indian tonic water

Squid Toast

500g strong white flour, plus extra for dusting
7g sachet fast-action dried yeast
1 tsp salt
350ml water (lukewarm)
sunflower oil (for greasing)
2 packets squid ink
900g loaf tin

Coral Mayonnaise

scallop roe powder (pinch of)
150ml mayonnaise

Red Grape Gimlet

200g red grapes
1 lime (juice of)
125ml Indian tonic water
50ml gin

Beetroot And Radish Crisps

1 raw candy beetroot
2 baby salad radishes
icing sugar (to dust)

1 large frisée lettuce

Chef's Tip

We use dried, ground scallop roe mixed with mayonnaise but, to save buying scallops, lemon and lime will work just as well in the mayonnaise, or even saffron.

Method

For The Salmon (Prepare the day before)
Mix the salt, sugar and juniper berries. Thoroughly cover the salmon in the salt mixture and refrigerate in a clingfilmed tray for at least 24 hours. Mix the lime juice, zest, tonic water and gin. Rinse the salmon, then marinate in the gin and tonic mixture for four hours. Remove the salmon from the marinade and pat dry. Cut into four pieces of equal length, then roll each piece individually in clingfilm tightly (like you would a sausage). Take each loose end of clingfilm and keep twisting the ends. The salmon should start to take on a cylinder shape. Return to the fridge to rest for four hours. When released from clingfilm, cut into three pieces and they are ready to serve.

For The Red Grape Gimlet
Blend all the ingredients and leave to infuse for around two to three hours. When infused, pour the mixture through a fine sieve. Serve in an espresso cup or shot glass.

For The Beetroot And Radish Crisps
Peel the candy beetroot and slice as thinly as possible. Slice the radishes to the same thickness. Place the vegetables on a tray lined with greaseproof paper and dust with icing sugar. Place in an oven at 60°C for around two hours or until crisp.

For The Squid Toast
Tip the flour, yeast and salt into a large bowl and make a well in the middle. Pour in most of the water and squid ink. Mix the flour and water together until combined to a slightly wet, pillowy, workable dough. Add a splash more water if necessary. Tip the dough onto a lightly floured surface and knead for at least ten minutes until smooth and elastic. This can also be done in a tabletop mixer with a dough hook. Place the dough in a clean, oiled bowl, cover with clingfilm and leave to rise until doubled in size. Heat an oven to 220°C/fan 200°C. Knock back the dough by tipping it back onto a floured surface and pushing the air out. Mould the dough into a rugby ball shape and place in the tin. Cover with a clean tea towel and leave to prove for 30 minutes. Dust the top of the loaf with a little more flour and slash the top with a sharp knife. Bake the bread for 15 minutes, then reduce the heat to 190°C/fan 170°C and continue to bake for 30 minutes until the loaf sounds hollow when removed from the tin and tapped on the base. Leave to cool completely. The loaf will stay fresh in an airtight container for three days or can be frozen for one month. Slice the bread as thin as you can and place in the oven at 60°C until dry and crisp.

For The Coral Mayonnaise
Mix the mayonnaise with the pinch of scallop roe powder.

To Serve
Plate as pictured.

SEARED FILLET OF STONE BASS, PARMENTIER POTATOES, CRISP SEAWEED, CLAMS & LEMONGRASS

SERVES 4

Pazo de Barrantes, Albarino
(Spain)

Ingredients

Fish

4 x 200g portions stone bass
4 tbsp oil
knob of butter
salt and pepper

4 sheets nori (dried seaweed)

Parmentier Potatoes

4 large baking potatoes
500g fresh clams (washed)
butter and oil (for frying)

Lemongrass Bisque

1 lobster shell
300g prawn shells
2 tbsp olive oil
$1/2$ lemon (juice of)
1 onion, or 2 shallots (chopped)
3 cloves garlic (crushed)
2 sticks celery (chopped)
2 carrots (chopped)
6 tomatoes (chopped)
5 sticks lemongrass (chopped)
3 kaffir lime leaves
1 tsp paprika
1 bay leaf
salt and pepper
2 glasses white wine
50g tomato purée
500ml double cream
few knobs of unsalted butter
salt and pepper

Method

For The Lemongrass Bisque

In a large saucepan, fry the lobster and prawn shells in a little olive oil for five minutes. Add the lemongrass and lime leaves. Add the chopped onion or shallots, garlic, celery and carrot and fry for a further five minutes. Add the chopped tomatoes, paprika, bay leaf and seasoning and stir well. Add the lemon juice, white wine, tomato purée and water to cover. Bring to a boil, then gently simmer for one hour, skimming the surface periodically to remove scum. Pass through a fine-meshed sieve. Return to saucepan and gently reduce to half the volume. Gently whisk in the double cream and butter until the sauce thickens. Add seasoning to taste.

For The Parmentier Potatoes

Peel and dice the potatoes to around 1cm. Place in a saucepan and cover with water. Bring to a boil, then simmer until you can insert a knife easily. Remove from the heat and run under cold water until cool. Drain. Place a little butter and oil in a frying pan and add the potatoes. Gently fry until golden, then add clams and sauté until the clams open.

> **Chef's Tip**
>
> Give the clams a tap on the side and if they are fresh they should close up, if they don't they are dead and should be discarded.

For The Crisp Seaweed

Dampen the seaweed sheet and place on a towel to remove excess water. Tear to desired shapes and carefully place in a deep fat fryer at 180°C until they stop fizzing. Remove from the fryer and place on some kitchen towel to remove excess grease.

For The Stone Bass

Heat a heavy bottomed frying pan, add four tablespoons of oil and a small knob of butter. Add the fish fillets to the pan, skin side-down, and season the flesh side. Leave to cook for two to three minutes until the flesh of the fish is opaque three quarters of the way up. At this point, turn the fish over and cook for a further two minutes.

To Serve

Plate as pictured.

DUCK EGG CUSTARD TART, GOOSEBERRY SORBET & GINGERBREAD

SERVES 10

🍷 *Ochoa Moscatel (Spain)*

Ingredients

Gooseberry Sorbet
250g gooseberries
400ml elderflower cordial
100ml water

Sweet Pastry
225g plain flour
110g butter
80g caster sugar
1 large egg
milk

Egg Custard
800ml double cream
12 duck egg yolks
200g caster sugar
1 vanilla pod (split lengthways)
1 nutmeg

Gingerbread
120g butter
120g dark soft sugar
240g black treacle
2 large eggs
220g self raising flour
2 tbsp ground ginger
2 tsp allspice

Garnish
raspberries
rhubarb purée (optional)

Method

For The Sweet Pastry
Crumb together, by hand, the butter into the flour. Add the sugar. Mix in the egg and enough milk to form a soft dough. Wrap in clingfilm and place in the fridge to rest for one hour. Preheat the oven to 200°C. Roll out the pastry and line a 25cm loose-bottomed flan tin, leaving any excess pastry to hang over the edge (do not trim until after the pastry has been cooked). Line with greaseproof paper and fill with baking beans or rice. Bake for eight to ten minutes. Remove from the oven. Remove the greaseproof paper and baking beans. Reduce the oven temperature to 180°C.

For The Egg Custard
Heat the cream and vanilla pod in a saucepan without letting it boil. In a bowl, beat the egg yolks and caster sugar for three to four minutes until pale and thick. Gradually whisk the hot cream into the mixture, being careful not to let the egg yolks curdle. Pour the mixture into the cooked pastry case. Bake for 40 minutes or until the custard is set. Remove from the oven, trim the edges carefully and allow to cool. Grate nutmeg over tart while still warm. Serve at room temperature.

For The Sorbet
Put the gooseberries in a pan with 200ml of the elderflower cordial and 100ml of the water and simmer for five minutes. Purée the mixture with the rest of the cordial, sieve and leave to cool. Churn in an ice cream maker for 30 minutes (or freeze for two hours, stir, freeze for four hours, then whizz in a food processor.) Return to the freezer for at least six hours, whichever method you use.

For The Gingerbread
In an electric mixer, cream the butter and sugar. In a microwave, slightly warm the treacle to soften it, then gently pour into the butter. Add the eggs, sieved flour and spices and gently mix in. Grease and flour a 28cm x 13cm loaf tin and pour in the gingerbread mixture. Bake at 150°C for 50 minutes. Remove from the oven and leave to cool. Once cooled, slice as thinly as possible. Place on a greaseproof sheet and bake in the oven at 60°C for one hour.

Chef's Tip
Crush some of the dried gingerbread to crumbs to use as a base to serve the sorbet on.

To Serve
Assemble as pictured with a swipe of rhubarb purée (optional).

052
BOUCHON BISTROT

4-6 Gilesgate, Town Centre, Hexham, NE46 3NJ

01434 609 943
www.bouchonbistrot.co.uk

Bouchon brings a little corner of rural France to Northumberland.

French owned and run, this is the classic country bistrot where you can close your eyes and the tastes, smells and sounds of France are yours. Our style is traditional; our signature menus features classics such as escargots with garlic and parsley butter, French onion soup, bouillaibaisse with sea bass and monkfish and crispy duck confit with lyonnaise potatoes. Our classic desserts include Armagnac and prune clafoutis, classic Ile Flottante and profiteroles au chocolat.

Our French onion soup represents the essence of France in a single bowl; a simple and traditional dish prepared, like all our food, expertly, confidently and with respect for every ingredient.

Our dishes, like our restaurant, are fresh and uncomplicated, created from the finest produce and served simply and in season in the traditional French country way.

Long, laid-back lunches, big family dinners or romantic dining à deux; our 18th Century home in the heart of Hexham's historic leather tanning and merchants' quarter is warm and intimate; a little corner of France in the Tyne Valley.

Alors bon appétit!

Relish Restaurant Rewards
See page 003 for details.

French owned and run, this is the classic country bistrot where you can close your eyes and the tastes, smells and sounds of France are yours.

PATE DE CAMPAGNE

SERVES 16

♈ *Marcillac 'Lo Sang del Païs' Domaine du Cros 2011
(France)*

Ingredients

1.5kg pork throat
1kg belly pork
50g salt
1 tsp white pepper (ground)
5 shallots
¼ bunch flat leaf parsley
3 eggs (including 1 for egg-wash)
300g *crépinette*
3 bay leaves

Method

Mince the pork throat and belly, shallots and flat leaf parsley together. Add the salt, pepper and two eggs. Mix well. Lay the *crépinette* inside a cast iron terrine mould – this will help the mix hold together during cooking. Add the mince, making sure you put a large amount in the terrine as it will shrink while cooking.

For presentation, as well as taste, lay the three bay leaves nicely on top of the terrine prior to cooking. Egg-wash the top of the terrine in order to get a nice, shiny finish. Use a *bain-marie* - an ovenproof container (large enough to hold the terrine) with water - and cook the terrine in an oven at 180°C for approximately one and a half hours.

Allow the terrine to cool down then refrigerate.

Bon appétit!

Chef's Tip

Best served at room temperature with toasted bread, small cornichons (gherkins) and most importantly, a nice glass of red wine, relatively light to medium.

JEROME'S BOUILLABAISSE!

SERVES 4

🍷 *A white wine with caractère, like a wine from the Rhône Valley, or a Roussane and Marsanne based white wine, or you can also look for a Bandol Rosé!*

Ingredients

Bouillabaisse

2 whole red mullet
2 whole sea bream
4 king prawns
1 fennel bulb (diced)
1 large onion (diced)
$^1/_2$ head (or bulb) garlic (crushed)
1 carrot (diced)
1 stick celery (diced)
$^1/_2$ tbsp tomato paste
2 pinches saffron
100ml white wine
4 ripe tomatoes (diced)
20g fennel seeds
2 bay leaves
1 sprig thyme

Garnish

4 baby fennel
12 new potatoes (peeled)
1 carrot (*turned*)
1 courgette (*turned*)
12 cherry tomatoes (on the vine)
1$^1/_2$ ltrs vegetable stock

Method

For The Bouillabaisse

Scale and fillet the fish, keeping the bones on the side for the sauce. Peel the prawns and remove the heads. Roast the fish bones in olive oil. Add the diced fennel bulb, the onion, crushed garlic, carrot, celery, fennel seeds, bay leaves and thyme. Sweat everything together, add the tomato paste and *deglaze* with the wine. Reduce until almost dry, then add water to cover the ingredients, a pinch of saffron and the diced tomatoes. Season to taste and cook for 20 minutes. Put the mixture through a moulis - a big potato masher - then through a sieve. Check seasoning and add more if necessary.

To Serve

Cook the peeled new potatoes in water with a pinch of saffron.

Braise the baby fennel in half of the vegetable stock. *Blanch* the carrots and courgettes in separate pans until 'al dente'. Transfer the vegetables to one pan and glaze for seven minutes in vegetable stock and butter to finish cooking and to give a nice shine to the vegetables.

Roast the cherry tomatoes in an 180°C oven. Keep on the vine for presentation.

Panfry the fish (skin side down) and prawns with olive oil in a non-stick pan. Season to taste.

Serve in a shallow plate, with the sauce and vegetables at the bottom - position the fennel at a 45° angle to add volume to the dish, then place the fish on top. Finish with the cherry tomatoes. Serve with a fork and a soup spoon and crusty bread to polish it off with!

And here you are, in Marseille, with the sun shining and your feet in the water!

TARTE AU CITRON & LAVANDE

SERVES 4

🍷 *Riesling Vendanges Tardives, Alsace (France)*

Ingredients

Sweet Pastry

250g plain flour
125g butter (softened)
100g sugar
1 egg yolk
water (drop of)

Lemon And Lavender Mixture

125g sugar
2 eggs
2 lemons (juice of)
25g butter
1 sprig dried lavender (or lavender syrup)

crème fraîche

Method

For The Sweet Pastry

To make the pastry dough, mix the flour, softened butter and sugar together, then add the yolk and water. Work the mix together, then wrap in clingfilm and let it rest for at least one hour in the fridge.

After one hour, roll down to 2mm (the thinner the better) and place in either individual moulds or a family size mould. Par-cook the pastry with a weight in the middle (we use uncooked rice) at 175°C for 15 minutes.

For The Lemon Mixture

Infuse the lavender in the lemon juice. Let it infuse for as long as you can, overnight if possible. Strain the juice when done. Break the eggs in a mixing bowl, add the sugar and beat until pale. Add the infused lemon juice, then the butter.
In a *bain-marie*, whisk the mix to get a thick texture (like a curd). Pour the mix into the cool pastry case/s and let it set.

To Serve

Serve with a *quenelle* of cold crème fraîche.

062
THE BRASSERIE

Malmaison Hotel, Quayside, Newcastle upon Tyne, NE1 3DX

08446 930 658
www.malmaison.com

 ituated at the foot of the Millennium Bridge and overlooking the quayside, Malmaison Newcastle has the perfect backdrop. The iconic building offers amazing views of the Tyne and, despite being right at the heart of Newcastle's great shops and exciting nightlife, the lure of Malbar's legendary cocktails and the Mal Brasserie's classic dishes with a twist, is pretty strong.

Head up to the bar for a pre-dinner drink. From there you can watch the world go by whilst perusing the menu. The heart and soul of every Malmaison hotel is The Brasserie, where iconic dishes are prepared with a modern twist and served with passion and personality. Offerings include sublime steaks, the awesome Mal Burger, locally inspired blackboard specials and a mouthwatering wine list.

At Malmaison Newcastle, portions are generous and the quality sky high, all thanks to our superstar chefs. We cater for all needs and tastes, in our classic cuisine with a Malmaison twist.

 Relish Restaurant Rewards
See page 003 for details.

"I joined Malmaison in the summer of last year and, along with our new general manager, we are building a passionate team in the kitchen and Brasserie who all believe in good food. While Newcastle has some fantastic restaurants, it doesn't have the food culture of many cities yet, so the team has taken some time to form.

I believe we are there and we have good strengths in many areas. All of the team believe in what we put on the plate. I have a young, keen team, eager to serve the best food. Because we are a small kitchen, everything from our ice creams to terrines or gnocchi really is a team effort!"

MAL LOLLIPOPS

SERVES 4

🍷 *Pinot Noir, Loredona, Monterey (serve slightly chilled) (USA)*

Ingredients

Crab And Apple Spring Rolls
100g white crabmeat
50g green apple (cut into small dice)
seasoning, 10ml lemon juice
50g crème fraîche, 1 tsp chives (chopped)
200g spring roll pastry
water and flour glue (10g flour and 5ml water)

Tempura Prawns
4 large tiger king prawns (peeled)
200ml iced water (quickly whisked)
50g plain flour, 50g potato flour, salt (pinch of)

Thai Fish Cake Bon Bons
100g fresh salmon (diced)
25g lemongrass (chopped)
fish sauce (splash of), 1tsp red chilli (chopped)
10ml lime juice, seasoning
2 tsp coriander (chopped)
100g risotto rice (cooked in 100ml fish stock
with lemongrass, lime leaf and dried chilli)
flour, 1 egg (beaten), Panko breadcrumbs, milk
(to coat)

Chicken Satay Skewers
1 chicken breast
6 tbsp light soy sauce
1 tbsp water
5g ginger, 5g chilli
coriander stalks (chopped) ,1 clove garlic

Thai Pork Balls
200g lean pork (minced very fine with a knife)
10ml fish sauce
soy sauce and sweet chilli sauce (splash of)
10g breadcrumbs (to bind)
1 spring onion (sliced very thin)
10g coriander (chopped), 5g mint (chopped)
10g cornflour, 25g sugar or palm sugar
1 red chilli (chopped), 1 lime (juice of)
flour, 1 egg (beaten), Panko breadcrumbs, milk
(to coat)

Thai Dipping Sauce
1 carrot, 1 cucumber, 1 chilli, 1 shallot (*brunoise*)
250g sugar, 2 tsp salt, 1cm piece galangal
120ml white malt vinegar
cornflour (enough to thicken)

Method

For The Crab Spring Rolls

Wearing gloves, pick the crab three times. If you can still find shell, pick again. Squeeze out any water and place in a bowl. Add the chives, seasoning, apple, lemon juice and crème fraîche - just enough to bind. Mix the flour and water to make a paste to glue the spring roll pastry.

Cut one sheet of spring roll pastry lengthways and trim off any uneven edges. Cut one third off the top and discard. Brush the bottom and sides with the flour and water paste. Place the crab mix at the bottom and roll up. When the crab mixture is covered, stop and paste the sides and top and fold in. Roll up tight and keep cool.

For The Thai Fish Cake Bon Bons

Mix all of the ingredients together (except for the rice) and marinate the salmon for one hour. Mix in the cooked rice with a wet hand and form into four small balls. Coat the balls first in flour, then egg, then milk and Panko breadcrumbs. Deepfry at 180°C until golden.

For The Satay Chicken (Prepare the day before)

Mix all of the ingredients together and marinate the chicken overnight. Take out of the fridge and chargrill.

For The Thai Pork Balls

Warm the sugar and all the liquid in a pan until the sugar dissolves. Cool, then mix with the rest of the ingredients. With wet hands, roll into walnut size balls. Chill, then breadcrumb as before. Fry but be careful not to burn. You may need to finish off in the oven to make sure the balls are cooked.

For The Thai Dipping Sauce

Blitz all the ingredients together (except the cornflour), but not too finely. Bring the mixture to a boil until it thickens slightly. Add the cornflour, then mix until it thickens again. Keep in the fridge until required.

For The Tempura Prawns

Combine the ingredients. Coat the prawns and deepfry for two to three minutes until golden brown.

To Serve

Serve on skewers with the Thai dipping sauce and some homemade sweet chilli sauce. Place the skewers gently into the food, about half way through - be careful not to go completely through the food.

Chef's Tip

All of the lollipops can be made in advance, even the day before, and cooked when required, which takes minutes. Serve at home on a chopping board with barbecue skewers for a sharing platter.

FILLET OF COLEY, SMOKED HADDOCK CHOWDER, LOCAL SHELLFISH & SAMPHIRE

SERVES 4

Chardonnay, Haystack, Journeys End
(South Africa)

Ingredients

Coley

4 x 175 g portions coley
rapeseed oil and butter (for frying)

Chowder

250g smoked haddock (natural dyed fillets)
500g live mussels
200g tiger prawns (shelled and deveined)
2 large shallots
200ml dry white wine
25ml cider vinegar
500ml double cream
lemon juice (squeeze of)
bay leaf
tarragon stalks
50g podded peas
50g fresh samphire (washed)

Vegetables

16 cocotte potatoes (balls of Maris Piper potato
- use a melon baller)
500g spinach (washed and picked)
knob of butter

Garnish

50g pea shoots

Method

For The Chowder

Finely dice the shallots. Sauté in a pan with the white wine, cider vinegar and herbs. Reduce by half. Remove the tarragon stalks, add the mussels and cover. When the mussels open, remove from the liquid and set aside. Add the cream, a little water to thin and the whole haddock pieces. Cook and reduce the cream. As it starts to thicken, add the prawns. After one minute, return the mussels to the pan, add the samphire and peas and return to a boil. Finally, adjust the acidity with a squeeze of lemon juice.

For The Fillet Of Coley

Panfry the coley fillets in a little rapeseed oil and a knob of butter. Turn after two minutes and lower the heat. Cook for a further two minutes, spooning the butter over as it fries. Remove from the pan with a fish slice and keep to one side on a tray.

For The Vegetables

Cook the spinach in a pan with a little water and a knob of butter. Keep moving the spinach around in the pan. When cooked, season with a little salt. Don't season before it's cooked. Place on the tray with the fish.

Cook the potatoes in a low fryer at 130°C until just soft in the middle. Remove and drain on kitchen paper. When ready to serve, cook at 180°C in the oven for a couple of minutes to colour.

To Serve

Place the spinach in the centre of large bowl. Place the fish carefully on top, spoon the chowder generously around with the pea shoots and potatoes.

LIME CHEESECAKE WITH CHOCOLATE GANACHE & PIMMS JELLY

SERVES 4

🍷 *Veuve Clicquot Brut Rose, NV Champagne (France)*

Ingredients

Cheesecake
500g full fat soft cream cheese
130g icing sugar
1 vanilla pod (scrape seeds from)
1 lime (zest and juice of)
1 leaf gelatine
300ml double cream

Biscuit Base
150g Digestive biscuits
75g butter (melted)

Lime Syrup
1 lime (juice and zest of)
100g caster sugar
100ml water

Chocolate Ganache
100g 53% dark chocolate
100ml double cream

Pimms Jelly
200ml Pimms
50g caster sugar
50g strawberries (diced)
25ml lemon juice
2 leaves gelatine

Garnish
strawberries

Method

For The Biscuit Base And Cheesecake
Crush the biscuits and melted butter. Combine thoroughly. Press down evenly into moulds of your choice. Cream together the cream cheese, icing sugar, scraped vanilla seeds, lime juice and zest. Soak the gelatine in cold water. Bring the double cream to a boil, then add the pre-soaked gelatine. Combine with the cream cheese mixture and place in your lined moulds on top of the biscuit base. Leave to set in the fridge for a couple of hours.

For The Ganache
Melt the chocolate and cream together over a low heat. Remove from the heat as the chocolate starts to melt. Stir until the chocolate is completely melted and combined with the cream. Pour into a measuring jug. Allow to cool slightly before pouring on top of the cheesecake to prevent the cheesecake from melting. Chill for 20 to 30 minutes before serving.

For The Lime Syrup
Boil the water and sugar together and reduce by a third. Add the lime juice and zest. Remove from heat.

For The Pimms Jelly
Soak the gelatine in cold water. Bring the rest of the ingredients to a boil to remove the alcohol and dissolve the sugar. Add the gelatine and stir. Pour out onto a tray and set in the fridge. When set, cut into large dice.

To Serve
Serve as pictured.

> **Chef's Tip**
> This can also be made in layers as a trifle, setting each layer before adding the next and crumbling the biscuit base on the top.

072
THE BROAD CHARE

25, Broad Chare, Quayside, Newcastle upon Tyne, NE1 3DQ

0191 211 2144
www.thebroadchare.co.uk

A new kind of 'old' pub, The Broad Chare offers all the best bits of a traditional ale-house - well-kept beer, honest food, friendly company, good cheer - with a fresh, modern touch. Nothing fancy, nothing fussy, just genuine warmth and an open-hearted welcome. A proper pub.

One of those pubs you thought had disappeared along with whistling milkmen and red telephone boxes. It's the result of a happy partnership between Terry Laybourne's 21 Hospitality Group and Live Theatre, one of the country's leading new writing theatres.

We're big on warmth, low on fussiness: stripped wood floors, high bar stools, painted brickwork and comfy leather banquettes. Sup your pint beside our polished-oak bar or tuck yourself away in the snug behind the frosted glass partition. You can hear yourself talk, concentrate on the crossword or nod off quietly in the corner.

We choose our beers for their quality, craftsmanship and interest. Our own label house ale 'The Writer's Block' is a lovely, hoppy pale ale from Wylam Brewery in the Tyne Valley. We have regularly changing guest ales, Guinness and West beers on tap, along with an eclectic range of bottled beers. Plus there are ciders galore, 12 wines by the glass and a quirky collection of whiskies.

Upstairs in the dining room it's all reassuringly simple with solid wood tables, sturdy schoolroom chairs and shiny brass coat-hooks

Lunchtimes and evenings, tuck in your napkin for handsome starters such as potted shrimps or crab on toast, hearty main courses like fish pie or steak and chips, and old-fashioned puddings. We offer daily specials, such as Friday's fish and chips, plus a platter of British cheeses. Eat upstairs or down, on your own or with friends, one course or four. It's your pub, you choose.

Relish Restaurant Rewards
See page 003 for details.

Our menus offer honest, home cooked food like pubs used to serve; tasty, satisfying and proudly British. You can enjoy a proper sit-down-at-the-table meal or, if you're more in the mood for grazing while nursing your pint, or you're a bit pushed for time, try our bar snacks. These are bar snacks with attitude: generous, full of flavour, deliberately tempting - hand-raised pork pies, Scotch eggs, cauliflower fritters - they're almost a meal in themselves. Why not order a selection and share with friends?

BAKED DUCK EGG, SLOW COOKED OXTAIL & RED WINE

SERVES 4

🍺 Beer: A dark weighty beer such as Fuller's London Pride
🍷 Wine: A young Rioja

Ingredients

Slow-cooked Oxtail

1 oxtail (trimmed of excess fat and cut into pieces)
60ml vegetable oil
60g butter
2 tbsp plain flour
salt and pepper
2 onions (chopped)
3 carrots (cut into small chunks)
2 celery sticks (cut into small chunks)
2 cloves garlic (peeled and chopped)
2 tbsp tomato purée
1 small bouquet garni
375ml Beaujolais or other soft red wine
600ml beef stock

Baked Duck Egg

4 duck eggs
60g button mushrooms
60g button onions (*blanched* 3 mins in boiling
salted water)
60g smoked bacon (cut into lardons)
2 tbsp parsley (chopped)

4 slices sourdough bread (to serve)

Method

For The Oxtail

Preheat the oven to 135°C. Season the oxtail with salt and pepper, then roll in flour, shaking off any excess. Heat the vegetable oil in a heavy casserole dish and brown the oxtail pieces on all sides. Drain off the oil and replace with butter, then add the vegetables to the casserole and continue cooking until golden. Add the tomato paste and cook for a further two minutes before adding the red wine. Bring to a boil and simmer to reduce by half. Add the bouquet garni and enough beef stock to cover, then bring back to a boil. Cover with a lid and transfer to the preheated oven until the meat is very tender, about three and a half hours. Lift the oxtail pieces from the liquor with a slotted spoon and set aside. Strain the sauce through a fine sieve into a clean saucepan and simmer to reduce to a coating consistency. Carefully remove the meat from the bone into large chunks, discarding any fat, and add to the sauce. Check the seasoning and adjust if necessary.

To Assemble

Adjust the oven to 140°C. Butter four ovenproof serving dishes and season with salt and pepper. Crack each duck egg into a dish, season with a little more salt and pepper, then spoon the braised oxtail around. Place in the oven for around eight minutes until the egg whites are set, but leaving the yolk soft. Meanwhile, dry fry the bacon in a non-stick frying pan before adding the button onions and mushrooms. Allow to brown gently. Check seasoning and stir in the chopped parsley. Remove the eggs from the oven when they are cooked and spoon the bacon, onion and mushroom mixture over the top, leaving the yolk exposed, coat with remaining sauce.
Serve immediately with freshly toasted sourdough bread.

ROASTED 'FLATTY' WITH BACON, MUSSELS & CIDER

SERVES 4

Beer: Cantillon Geuze
Wine: Unoaked Chardonnay

Ingredients

Roasted Flatty

4 (approx 500g) super-fresh flat fish
(lemon sole, plaice or flounder - cleaned,
de-scaled and head removed - a good
fishmonger will happily do this for you)
1 lemon
salt and pepper
knob of butter

Mussels

600g fresh mussels (cleaned)
1 shallot (peeled and cut into large dice)
1 small carrot (peeled and cut into large dice)
1 clove garlic (peeled and crushed)
1 small sprig thyme
100ml dry cider

Sauce

180g smoked streaky bacon (cut into dice)
1 handful samphire (tough stalks removed)
140g butter
2 tbsp double cream
lemon (squeeze of)
black pepper

To Serve

broccoli and new potatoes (to serve)

Method

For The Mussels

Heat a medium-sized saucepan and, when hot, throw in the mussels, shallot, carrot, garlic, thyme and cider. Cover with a tight fitting lid and cook briefly until the mussels open. Remove the mussels from the pan with a slotted spoon. Set eight aside and remove the remainder from their shells. Strain the cooking liquor through a muslin and set aside.

For The Flatty Fish

Heat the olive oil in a large, non-stick frying pan (with an ovenproof handle). Season the fish and then place, white skin down, into the pan. Cook gently until golden, then cook in the oven for four to six minutes. Finish with a knob of fresh butter and a squeeze of lemon juice.

For The Sauce

Blanch the samphire in boiling water, without salt, for two minutes. Refresh in iced water then drain. Fry the diced bacon in a saucepan for three to four minutes until it begins to crisp. Pour in the mussel cooking liquor and simmer to reduce by half. Add the double cream, then whisk in the butter a little at a time. Season with a squeeze of lemon and a good grind of black pepper. Return all of the mussels and the samphire to the sauce and set aside to keep warm.

To Serve

Serve the flatty on a warm plate and spoon the bacon and mussel sauce around. Serve with steamed sprouting broccoli and some buttery new potatoes.

STEAMED APPLE & BLACKBERRY PUDDING

SERVES 4

🍷 *Nuy White Muscadel*
(Western Cape, South Africa)

Ingredients

Apple Compote

150g butter
100g sugar
1 Bramley apple

Pudding

150g caster sugar
3 eggs
170g unsalted butter (softened)
170g self-raising flour
8g baking powder
1 lemon (finely grated zest and juice of)
16 blackberries
60g apple compote (recipe above)

Custard

6 egg yolks
110g caster sugar
500g full fat milk
1 vanilla pod (split and seeds removed)

4 x 170ml pudding basins

Method

For The Apple Compote

Peel and core the apple and cut into 1.5cm chunks. Melt the butter in a stainless steel saucepan, then add the sugar. Allow the sugar to melt before throwing in the diced apples. Allow to cook uncovered, stirring from time to time, until the apples are tender. Remove from heat and allow to cool.

For The Custard

Heat the milk with half of the sugar, the vanilla pod and seeds. Whisk the eggs yolks and remaining sugar in a bowl until white and thickened slightly. When the milk boils, pour half of it onto the yolks and mix until smooth, then tip this into the remaining milk in the pan. Return to a low heat and cook, stirring continuously with a wooden spoon, until the mixture thickens enough to coat the back of the spoon (alternatively use a digital thermometer and cook to 82°C). Set aside and keep warm.

For The Pudding

Sieve the flour and baking powder together. Whisk the eggs. Gently warm the sugar in the oven and then shower into the eggs. Continue whisking until the mixture is white and at a ribbon consistency. Add the butter in small pieces, a little at a time. Fold in the sifted flour, followed by the grated lemon zest and juice. Butter and flour four 170ml individual pudding basins and place four blackberries in the base of each, followed by a tablespoon of apple compote. Fill almost to the brim with the sponge mixture and cover each loosely with a piece of buttered foil. Steam for 45 minutes, then allow to rest for five minutes, before turning out into dessert bowls. Serve with a jug of hot custard.

082
CAFE 21

Trinity Gardens, Quayside, Newcastle upon Tyne, NE1 2HH

0191 222 0755
www.cafetwentyone.co.uk

With sleek, social and seriously good food, Café 21 is bursting with city centre buzz and a culinary reputation to match.

This isn't the stuff of sober suits and formality though. Style may be sharp, but the mood is relaxed. Service is sassy but never fussy. The food is skillful but designed to satisfy.

The atmosphere is bright; the décor is cool, but the greeting and service is genuinely warm. Whether you're booted and suited and entertaining business clients, calling in for a casual cocktail or coffee, or out celebrating a special occasion, everyone is met with a smile and encouraged to relax and enjoy their stay.

Chic, sharp, fun - the vibe is easy and unhurried; linger on a stool by the bar, drink a cocktail, browse the menu and anticipate. The food will delight.

Dishes are big on flavour; classics and contemporary alike. Nothing is left to chance; our fresh, seasonal ingredients are carefully sourced and treated with respect.

Whether you're ladies that lunch or businessmen that dine, there's a range of menu options. Vegetarians can also enjoy an extensive range of dishes that are given the same attentive preparation as our meat and seafood.

For private groups, business or social, our private dining room is like a restaurant within our restaurant; stylish, modern and flexible, ideal for formal or informal meetings, lunches or dinners.

Relish Restaurant Rewards
See page 003 for details.

WARM CHOCOLATE POT WITH CHURROS

SERVES 4

A glass of Banyuls Rimage Rouge, from Abbé Rous, South West France. The wine needs to cut through the richness of the chocolate without being cloying on the palate.

Ingredients

Churros

250ml water
90g unsalted butter
175g plain flour
caster sugar (pinch of)
salt (pinch of)
2 medium eggs (beaten)

Chocolate Pot

330ml double cream
1 vanilla pod
1 cinnamon stick
165g best quality dark chocolate (grated - we use Valrhona Araguani 72%)
20g semi-whipped cream

Method

For The Churros

Bring the water and butter to a boil in a medium saucepan. Remove from the heat and add the flour and salt. Return to a low heat and beat with a spatula until the mixture comes together, is smooth and begins to come away from the side of the pan. Remove the pan once more from the heat and leave the mixture to cool slightly. Beat in the eggs, a little at a time. Transfer the mixture to a piping bag fitted with a 20mm star nozzle and pipe into 150mm lengths on non-stick baking paper.

For The Chocolate Pot

Split the vanilla pod lengthways and scrape out the seeds, using a small knife. Bring the cream to a boil with the vanilla seeds, pod and the cinnamon. Remove from the heat and leave to infuse. Remove the vanilla pod and cinnamon stick. Return to the gas and re-heat gently, then stir in the grated chocolate (retaining one tablespoon to garnish) until melted. Add the semi-whipped cream then strain into a warmed jug, then share between small glasses or espresso cups.

To Assemble

Heat a deep fat fryer to 180°C. Cut the paper around the churros then, using the paper, lower them carefully into the hot fat. Fry for three to four minutes until golden, keeping them moving with a spoon all the while. Remove with a slotted spoon, drain on absorbent paper, then toss in caster sugar. Serve immediately with the chocolate pot. Serve four or five hot churros on a plate lined with a napkin. Place a pot of chocolate cream alongside for dunking

NB: If necessary, the chocolate cream can be re-heated gently in a microwave just before serving.

092
THE CAFE ROYAL

8 Nelson Street, Newcastle upon Tyne, NE1 5AW

0191 231 3000
www.caferoyalnewcastle.co.uk

This stylish café bistro, in the historic heart of Newcastle, offers all day dining in comfortable, social surroundings and beautiful Georgian architecture.

The key to head chef Cevat Robert Elat's food is fresh ingredients sourced on our doorstep. His aim is to transfer his passion for food on to every plate and include new and interesting flavours and combinations in his dishes.

This contemporary café bistro is a relaxing haven, a social hub where you can truly indulge your taste buds. Breakfast, morning coffee, lunch and afternoon tea can all be enjoyed within this chic interior. Fused with Café Royal's grand, neo-classical façade, it makes this a truly special place.

Under the guidance of food development manager, Adrian Watson, all menus feature freshly prepared, seasonal dishes with specials changing weekly.

This encompasses the in-house bakery, which produces the freshest croissants, pastries, tray bakes, artisan bread and cakes, all made with the finest ingredients and only available at Café Royal.

Relish Restaurant Rewards
See page 003 for details.

cheeses, wine & olives, coffee
olives, oils & vinegars

organics, coffee
oils & vinegars

Our chefs continue to break new grounds with recognition nationally for high quality and standards produced and delivered by Cevat's team. The inspiration for the stunning dishes and amazing food comes through continual development via the Sir John Fitzgerald's Chef School held at the Café Royal.

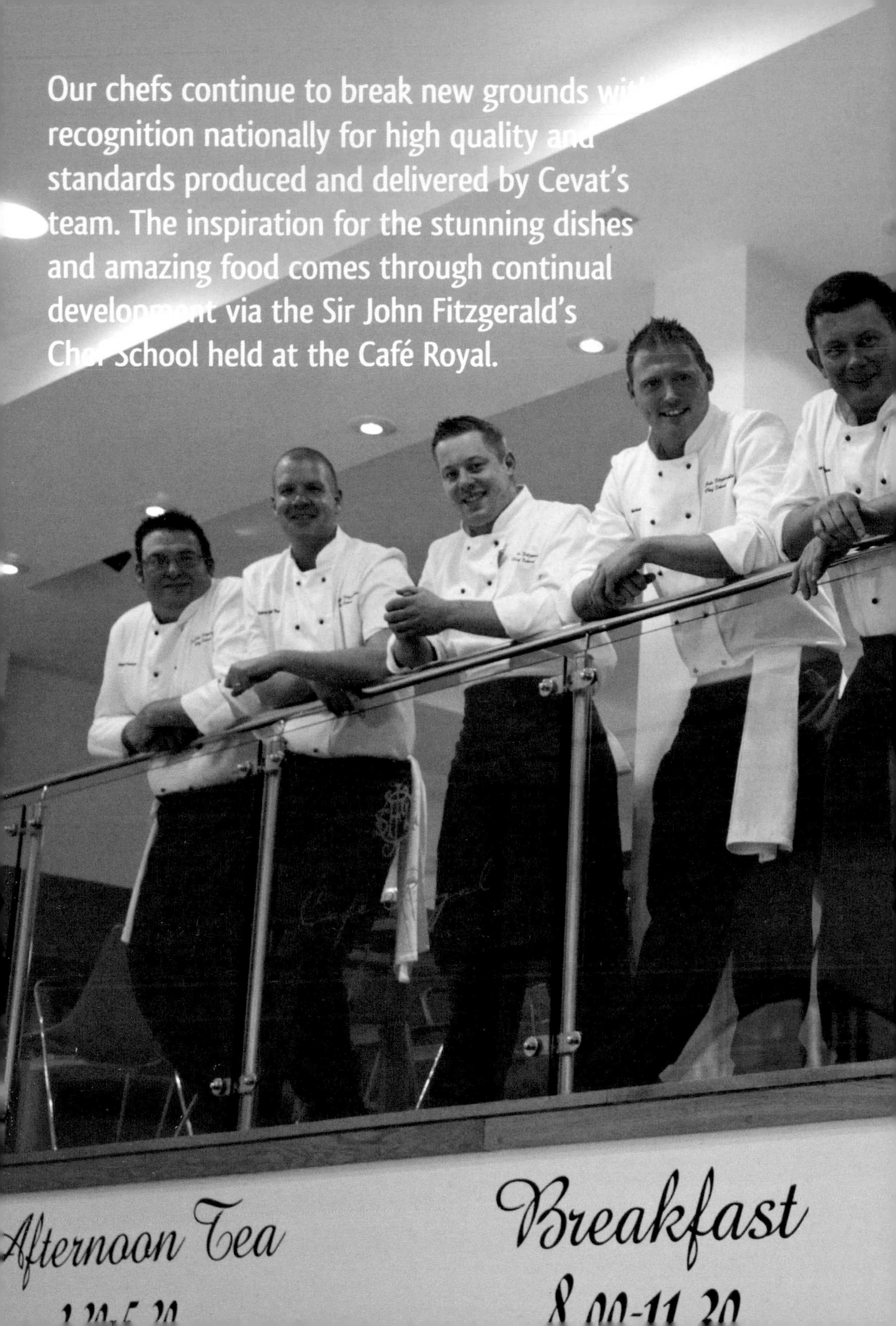

Afternoon Tea

Breakfast

8.00-11.30

Café Royal

From our Kitc

12.00 - 5.30

YELLISON GOAT'S CHEESE, ROASTED RED PEPPER, GOLDEN BEETROOT PESTO, RAW HONEY & SAFFRON

SERVES 4

La Croix du Roy Sancerre 2010
(France)

Ingredients

2 Yellison goat's cheese rolls
2 red peppers (roasted)
oil, thyme and garlic (for roasting)

Golden Beetroot Pesto
6 golden beetroots
1ltr mineral water
2 cloves garlic, 3 sprigs thyme
1 lemon (peeled)
90g pine nuts (toasted)
5g Reggiano Parmiggiano
75ml arachide oil

Pickled Golden Beetroot
6 golden beetroot (cooked in white balsamic pickling liquor and cut into desired shapes)

Gazpacho Dressing
5 plum tomatoes
4 red peppers (seeds removed and finely chopped)
3 red onions (peeled and finely chopped)
10 spring onions (finely chopped)
2 cloves garlic (finely chopped)
2 cucumbers (peeled and de-seeded)
2 tbsp tomato purée
2 tbsp red wine vinegar, 1 tbsp Worcester sauce
salt and pepper
1 bunch flat leaf parsley (finely chopped)
1 bunch chives (finely chopped)

Lemon Infused Feuilles de Brick
1 sheet feuilles de brick pastry
1tsp lemon oil

Raw Wicken Fen Honey Dressing
100ml raw Wicken Fen honey
6 stamens saffron

Garnish
rocket flowers, apple marigold leaves
baby red pak choi shoots

Method

Crumble the goat's cheese into a bowl, then weigh out into four 70g portions. Place three sheets of clingfilm onto a cold surface and form the portions of crumbled goat's cheese into cylinders, rolling up the clingfilm tightly. Allow to set in the fridge. Roast the red peppers with the oil, thyme and garlic, then skin and cut into oblong shapes.

> **Chef's Tip**
> Take care in making the Yellison all the same size and allow enough time for them to set properly in a refrigerator.

For The Pesto

Place the garlic, thyme, lemon and beetroots into a stainless steel pan and cover with the mineral water. Bring to a simmer and cook for ten to 15 minutes until tender. Allow to cool in the cooking liquor. Peel off the beetroots' outer skins, revealing their vibrant colour. Place in a hot mix pro, or food processor, and blend with the pine nuts, parmesan and oil. Season to taste. Pass through a fine *chinois*.

For The Gazpacho Dressing

Blend the tomatoes, peppers, onion, spring onions, garlic, cucumber and herbs to a fine pulp. Add the liquids and blend again. Pass through a fine *chinois* and season to taste .

For The Feuilles de Brick

Cut the pastry into four 8cm long 3cm wide pieces. Rub with the lemon oil and roll around a stainless steel ring to form tubes. Cook at 180°C for four minutes until golden. Remove from the ring whilst still warm and set aside to cool. Store in an airtight container until needed.

For The Honey Dressing

Boil 30ml of the honey. Add the saffron strands and allow to infuse for 24 hours. Finish by adding the remaining raw honey.

To Serve

Place the oblong pepper onto a flat, round, white plate and top with the feuilles de brick tube. Remove the goat's cheese from the clingfilm and carefully place inside the pastry cylinder. Glaze the goat's cheese with a gas gun to caramelise slightly. Dot the plate with beetroot pesto and gazpacho sauce and garnish with rocket flowers, apple marigold leaves and baby red pak choi. Finish with a drizzle of the honey saffron dressing.

ROASTED SPRING LAMB RUMP, VALLUM FARM BABY VEGETABLES, JERSEY ROYALS, MINT OIL

SERVES 4

🍷 *Peregrine Pinot Noir, 2010*
(New Zealand)

Ingredients

Spring Lamb
4 x 150g spring lamb rumps
4 cloves garlic (sliced)
8 sprigs wild thyme
4 tbsp arachide oil
Himalayan salt and white pepper (to season)
40g butter

Carrot Purée
10 Vallum Farm carrots (peeled and sliced very thinly)
500ml carrot juice
salt and pepper (to season)

Pea Purée
500g fresh peas (in pods)
ice cubes

Mint Oil
200g mint leaves (picked)
200ml pommace oil
50g parsley (picked)

Jersey Royals
200g Jersey Royals
4 cloves garlic
2 sprigs thyme
6 stalks parsley
4 white peppercorns
1 bay leaf
salt and pepper
1ltr mineral water

Garnish
seasonal micro vegetables
white balsamic vinegar
Ken Hollands mirco herbs and shoots
rich red wine sauce (optional)
podded peas
garlic flowers

Method

For The Spring Lamb
Prepare the spring lamb rumps by trimming off the outer membrane, leaving a layer of flavoursome fat intact. Drop each lamb rump into its own individual sous-vide bag with two sprigs of the thyme, one clove of garlic and one tablespoon of oil. Water bath the lamb for 25 minutes at 66°C. Blast chill. Alternatively, use a pan and thermometer and keep checking.

Remove the lamb from the bags and season with Himalayan salt and freshly ground white pepper. Sear on all sides until caramelised and golden brown. Cook for approximately seven minutes, basting all the time with nut-brown butter. Set to one side, allowing the meat to rest.

> **Chef's Tip**
> If you allow the meat to rest for at least three to four minutes this relaxes the meat, making it more tender.

For The Carrot Purée
Bring the carrot juice and carrots to a boil in a saucepan. Reduce until the liquid has become syrupy. Check the carrots are cooked. Place the carrots and juice into a Hot Mix Pro, or food processor, and blend until smooth. Pass through a fine *chinois*, then whisk over ice until cold. Season to taste.

For The Pea Purée
Pod and *blanch* the peas. Drain off the water blend in a Hot Mix Pro, or food processor. Add one ice cube at a time until you reach the desired consistency. Pass through a fine *chinois*, then whisk over ice until cool. Season to taste.

For The Mint Oil
Blanch the herbs in boiling water. Refresh in iced-water and squeeze out any excess water. Blend with the oil in a Hot Mix Pro, or food processor, taking the temperature to 60°C. Pass through a *chinois* and whisk until cool over ice.

For The Jersey Royals
Place all of the ingredients in a heavy bottomed pan and bring to a simmer. Cook the potatoes until tender, then allow to cool in the liquor. Peel off the skins and warm gently to serve.

To Serve
Cut the lamb into the required shape, as pictured. Arrange the seasonal micro vegetables dipped in white balsamic vinegar, onto the plates. Add the warmed, peeled Jersey Royals. Garnish with podded peas, the two purées and Ken Holland's micro herbs and shoots. Finish with garlic flowers and an optional rich red wine sauce.

AFTERNOON TEA

SERVES 4

🍷 *A glass of Perrier Jouet Champagne*
(France)

Ingredients

Mini Eclairs

110g plain flour
175ml water
$^1/_2$ tsp salt
75g butter
3 eggs
vanilla pastry cream (to fill)
dark chocolate (melted, to coat)

Macaroons

175g icing sugar
125g ground almonds
3 large egg whites
75g caster sugar
colouring and flavouring or your choice

Macaroon Filling

150g butter (softened)
75g icing sugar
colouring and flavouring or your choice

Jersey Clotted Cream, Madagascan Vanilla And Yorkshire Strawberry Eton Mess

4 tbsp clotted cream
$^1/_2$ tsp Madagascan vanilla pod seeds
1 tbsp icing sugar
2 tbsp broken vanilla meringue pieces
4 large, plump, juicy Yorkshire strawberries (halved)
micro mint (picked)

Method

For The Mini Eclairs

Place the water, salt and butter into a heavy bottomed pan over a medium heat. Bring to a boil, then remove from the heat. Add the flour to the pan, stirring constantly with a spoon until combined. Return to the heat and beat until smooth and the paste comes away from the side of the pan. Remove from the heat and add the eggs, one at a time, stirring thoroughly.

Preheat an oven to 180°C. Fill a piping bag with the mixture and pipe out 18 éclairs, approximately 6cm long x 2.5cm wide, onto a buttered baking sheet. Bake for approximately 30 minutes until golden and cooked through. Cool on a wire rack. Fill with vanilla pastry cream (crème pâtissiere) and dip in melted dark chocolate, covering the whole length of the éclair.

For The Macaroons

Preheat the oven to 160°C. Whizz the almonds and icing sugar in a food processor to make a very fine powder. Whisk the egg whites in a separate bowl, with a touch of salt, to form soft peaks. Whisk in the caster sugar until thick and glossy. At this point, stir in the colour and flavouring of your choice. Fold in half of the almond and icing sugar mixture into the meringue and mix well. Fold in the remaining half until shiny, with a thick ribbon-like texture. Place in a piping bag fitted with a plain 1cm nozzle. Pipe rounds, about 3cm in diameter, onto baking sheets lined with baking paper. Leave to stand for 15 minutes until a skin forms, then bake for 15 minutes. Remove from the oven and cool.

For The Macaroon Filling

Beat together the butter and sugar, then add any flavouring and colour of your choice. Use to sandwich together two of the macaroons.

For The Eton Mess

Knock the clotted cream back with the icing sugar and vanilla. Fold in the meringue pieces and strawberries. Place into individual kilner serving jars. Finish with halved strawberries and picked micro mint.

> **Chef's Tip**
>
> Taste everything you make. Use only the best seasonal fruits available.

102
CAFFE VIVO

27 Broad Chare, Quayside, Newcastle upon Tyne, NE1 3DQ

0191 232 1331
www.caffevivo.co.uk

T he essence of an Italian neighbourhood cafe, slap bang in the heart of the city. Caffè Vivo is a rare experience; conviviality and ease are assured in the buzzy quayside surroundings. There is no standing on ceremony here and we welcome everyone, whether for a nourishing meal or a relaxing drink. The atmosphere is warm, easy going and fun. Drop by for a reviving cappuccino or spin out the time and talk over some tasty food - generous, joyful and full of Italian sunshine.

You can tuck yourself in a corner or come with a crowd of friends; there's nothing better than gathering together to enjoy some antipasto on our 'planks to share'. There's spicy, herby salamis, flavoursome pecorino and taleggio cheeses, or tasty vegetarian antipasto.

Try a freshly prepared pasta dish, a seafood treat or grilled meat from the main menu; otherwise there's the lunchtime specials, including an express lunch for those at work or with an appointment in the afternoon. Every day there's a special or two, which often features freshly caught, seasonal fish.

Caffè Vivo is gloriously relaxed; a former warehouse, with brick walls and cast-iron pillars, our style is casual, stylish and a little boho.

You can enjoy a Bellini, a light, fresh glass of wine, or chill with one of our cool Italian beers. There's no rush, just enjoy the visit.

Relish Restaurant Rewards
See page 003 for details.

Caffè Vivo is all about simple, authentic, Italian food, cooked with panache and passion. Our dishes are bold, honest and true to their ingredients. We get excited when the new season's produce arrives and our menus reflect this. Expect bright and sunny flavours, a dollop of rustic charm, a flash of Italian brio. Expect to feel nourished and loved.

PAPPARDELLE WITH SPRING VEGETABLES

SERVES 4

🍷 *Fiano from MandraRossa
(Sicily)*

A crisp white wine with a little bit of richness on the finish

Ingredients

320g egg pappardelle

Vegetable Stock

100g leeks (the white and light green only, finely sliced, washed and drained)
100g garlic (peeled and sliced)
3 shallots
100g butter
1 clove
1 bay leaf
6 white peppercorns
1ltr water
sea salt

Minted Pea Purée

400ml vegetable stock
500g frozen peas
1 sprig mint
salt (pinch of)
$^1/_2$ tsp sugar
$^1/_2$ tsp mint leaves (chopped)
20g unsalted butter

Vegetables

4 sticks asparagus (peeled)
90g fresh peas (podded)
90g broad beans (podded)
90g young courgette (cut into 3mm thick rounds)
1 handful young salad spinach (or rocket, washed)
1 punnet pea shoots
100g unsalted butter (cut into cubes)
salt and ground black pepper

To Serve

2tbsp mature pecorino (grated)
120g minted pea purée (recipe above)

Method

For The Vegetable Stock

Place everything together in a stainless steel saucepan and bring to a boil. Skim and simmer for 25 minutes. Remove from the heat and allow to cool before straining. Season with a little sea salt.

For The Minted Pea Purée

Bring the vegetable stock to a boil, then add the peas, mint sprig, salt and sugar. Cook until tender, then remove the sprig of mint. Liquidise the peas with half of their cooking liquor. Add enough of the remaining cooking liquor to create a smooth, silky sauce. Add the butter, then transfer to a bowl over ice to cool quickly. Stir in the chopped mint.

For The Vegetables

Cook the asparagus in boiling salted water until al dente. Remove with a slotted spoon and refresh in iced water. Repeat with the peas, courgettes and broad beans, removing the fine outer shell from the beans. Cut the asparagus on a bias into 3mm thick slices and place in a large flat pan together with the peas and broad beans. Season with a grind of pepper.

Take a ladle of pasta cooking water and add it to the pan of vegetables, bringing it rapidly to a boil. Add the butter, three or four cubes at a time, and 'swirl' the pan around to create a nice buttery emulsion. Check the seasoning and adjust if necessary, then throw in the spinach leaves and remove the pan from the heat until the pasta is ready.

To Serve

Bring a large pot of salted water to a boil and throw in the pappardelle. Cook until al dente, checking every two to three minutes. Drain the pasta and add to the pan with the vegetables. Shower in two thirds of the grated cheese. Toss gently, or mix carefully using tongs. Ladle a portion of the warm pea purée onto each plate and distribute the pasta evenly. Should there be any sauce remaining in the pan, simply spoon this over the top.

CALVES LIVER WITH SAGE, PINE NUTS & RAISINS

SERVES 4

🍷 *Chianti Superiore, Santa Cristina, Antinori from Tuscany for a classic match or Barbera d'Asti, Fiulot, again from Antinori but this time their estate in the Piedmont (Italy)*

Method

Heat two non-stick frying pans with the vegetable oil. Season the liver and place two slices in each pan. Cook over a medium heat for three minutes or so, then turn. Cook for a further three to four minutes, depending on how you like your liver cooked. Transfer to a warm tray.

Tip the oil from the pans and replace with butter. Heat until the butter foams, then throw in the sage leaves, pine nuts and sultanas. Return the liver to the pan and swirl everything around a little in order for the flavours to mingle. Add the capers. Remove the pans from the heat and divide their contents between four warmed plates. Discard the fat from the pan then return to the heat, adding the vinegar. Boil until reduced by half, then add the veal stock and bring to a boil. Finish by adding a knob of butter to each pan to enrich the sauce. Check for seasoning and pour around the liver.

To Serve

Serve as pictured with green vegetables and soft polenta (or potato purée).

> **Chef's Tip**
> Ask your butcher to cut the liver into 1cm thick slices. It's often cut too thinly, which often leads to over cooking.

Ingredients

Liver

4 x 1cm thick slices calves' liver
2 tbsp vegetable oil
50g butter
salt and pepper
12 sage leaves
3 tbsp pine nuts (toasted)
3 tbsp golden raisins ('plumped' in a little warm water and drained)
1 tbsp capers
60ml balsamic vinegar
100ml veal stock or brown chicken stock

To Serve

green vegetables
soft polenta (or potato purée)

PANNA COTTA WITH RASPBERRIES

SERVES 4

🍷 *Passito di Noto, Planeta
(Sicily)*

Ingredients

450ml double cream
110ml milk
1 vanilla pod
2 leaves gelatine
45ml Grappa
110g caster sugar
250g raspberries

4 x 170ml Dariole moulds

Method

Put the gelatine to soften in a bowl of cold water. Pour the cream and milk into a stainless steel, heavy bottomed saucepan. Split the vanilla pod lengthways and scrape the seeds into the cream. Bring to a boil, then lower the heat and simmer for five minutes to reduce slightly. Remove from the heat and stir in the sugar, the softened gelatine and 25ml of the grappa. Pour into a jug, and divide the mixture between four individual 170ml Dariole moulds. Refrigerate for three hours to set. Turn the desserts out by dipping the moulds into hot water for two seconds and inverting onto individual plates.

To Serve
Scatter the raspberries around, then pour the remaining Grappa directly over the panna cotta.

CASTLE EDEN INN

Stockton Road, Castle Eden, Hartlepool, Cleveland, TS27 4SD

01429 835 137
www.castleedeninn.com

Situated in the picturesque village of Castle Eden, the Castle Eden Inn is a traditional coaching inn dating back to the 18th Century, which has been transformed into a Michelin-guided eatery.

Since being lovingly restored in 2009, the inn has established a renowned reputation, receiving excellent reviews from both customers and the media, and is now considered one of the most talked about restaurants in the North East. It continues to go from strength to strength under the guidance of Masterchef finalist and head chef David Coulson.

David has worked hard to promote locally sourced produce at all times and is insistent on using only the best local suppliers to construct his menu. Whether it be spring lamb from Martin Anderson's farm up the road, game supplied by local gamekeeper Phil, or fish fresh from the boat, David is determined to keep the emphasis on the menu being individual. And, with his own creative style, he is more than happy to work with his customers to create something unique to them for a special occasion.

The Castle Eden Inn is a wonderful place to indulge and discover, be it to experience the exquisite à la carte menu David has created, a traditional Sunday lunch or to sample their 'Fish Market Friday' choices. Customers also have the choice of the daily specials menu, delivered fresh that morning, or the extensive bar menu on offer throughout the day. What we like to refer to as complex simplicity leads to fantastic flavours that entice the customer and take them on an appealing journey through starter, main and dessert.

The exceptional food is complemented by a large and varied range of real ales, wines, Champagnes and spirits and now a selection of cocktails and an extensive beer garden.

The Castle Eden Inn welcomes everyone seven days a week to relax, socialise and enjoy David, and his team's, creations. Be sure to ask what Ermelito the pâtisserie chef has on offer, from the baked Alaska to a selection of homemade ice creams, which can include some interesting flavours such as apricot jam or even Newcastle Brown Ale.

Relish Restaurant Rewards
See page 003 for details.

Since being lovingly restored in 2009, the inn has established a renowned reputation, receiving excellent reviews from both customers and the media, and is now one of the most talked about restaurants in the North East.

SCALLOP, PORK PIE, APPLE & PEA CRACKLING SALAD

SERVES 4

 *Muscadet Servre-et-Maine Sur Lie, Guillaume Charpentier (Loire, France)*

Ingredients

4 scallops

Pork Pie

1 sheet rolled puff pastry
2 butcher's sausages
5 slices pancetta
English mustard
herbs (finely chopped)
egg wash

Salad

1 pork or pork belly skin
1 Granny Smith apple (chopped)
2 plum tomatoes (chopped)
fine herbs
handful fresh peas

Garnish

5 slices pancetta (cooked)
sundried tomatoes (chopped)

Mushy Peas (Optional)

100g dried marrow fat peas (soaked overnight)
2g bicarbonate of soda
200g fresh peas
salt (pinch of)
vinegar (splash of)
knob of butter

rapeseed oil

Method

For The Pork Pies

Break the sausage and finely chop the pancetta. Mix together with some fine herbs and English mustard. Wrap the uncooked rough pastry around the raw chopped meat and coat in mixed egg. Make the mini pies, as in the picture, and cook for 20 minutes at 180°C.

For The Mushy Peas (Optional)

Boil the marrow fat peas with the bicarbonate of soda, salt, vinegar and butter until they form a mushy texture.

For The Scallops

Preheat the pan and add a little oil. Panfry the scallops until medium rare - approximately one and a half minutes each side. Rest for one minute.

For The Salad

Cook the pork skin in hot oil, in a very hot oven, until crispy. Serve with the chopped apple, handful of peas, tomatoes and fine herbs.

To Serve

Assemble dish as shown in the picture.

BEEF, BROCCOLI & OYSTER SAUCE, YORKSHIRE PUDDING POWDER

SERVES 4

Pint of Black Sheep Bitter – Riggwelter (United Kingdom)

Ingredients

2 heads broccoli

Beef

800g centre cut beef fillet
salt and cracked black pepper
2 knobs of butter

Tempura Oysters

4 oysters (*shucked*)
50g cornflour
20ml soda water (ice cold)
salt (pinch of)

Oyster Sauce

8 oysters (*shucked*)
2 tbsp oyster sauce
200ml reduced beef stock

Yorkshire Puddings

4 eggs
300ml milk
500g plain flour

Garnish

wild garlic leaves and flowers
mustard garlic leaves and flowers

Method

For The Broccoli

Using a spiralizer, prepare the broccoli spaghetti from one of the broccoli stalks. Cut the other broccoli stalk into ribbons. Cut the broccoli heads into florets and keep any remaining green to decorate. Serve raw.

For The Oysters

Shuck the oysters. Keep eight aside. Make the tempura batter by whisking together the cornflour, soda water and salt. Deep fry the four oysters in the tempura batter until crisp.

For The Oyster Sauce

Add the oyster sauce and oysters, with their juices, to the beef stock and warm. Be cautious not to over cook the oysters.

For The Yorkshire Puddings

Whisk the egg, flour and milk to make a smooth batter consistency. Chill until ready to cook. Pour the batter into piping hot oil in a Yorkshire pudding tray. Cook at 200°C for 20 minutes. Return to the oven 20 minutes just before serving to dry out. When brittle, crumble the puddings.

> **Chef's Tip**
> Crumble the Yorkshire pudding at the last second in order to maintain the aroma.

For The Beef

Season the beef fillet with salt and cracked black pepper. Seal in a red hot pan on all sides. Add a couple knobs of butter and roast in a hot oven at 220°C for ten minutes (for medium rare). Rest for ten minutes.

To Serve

Cut the beef into into four equal pieces. Arrange the elements as pictured and garnish with the garlic and mustard leaves and flowers.

CHOCOLATE BROWNIE & SALTED CARAMEL ALASKA

SERVES 4

Aleatico Passito, A Mano
(Puglia, Italy)

Ingredients

18cm x 7cm baking tin

Brownie

185g butter
185g high quality dark chocolate (in chunks)
85g plain flour
40g cocoa powder
50g white chocolate (in chunks)
50g milk chocolate (in chunks)
3 large eggs
275g caster sugar

Italian Meringue

200g caster sugar
200ml cold water
5 egg whites
cream of tartar (pinch of)

Ice Cream

300g caster sugar
50g salted butter
5 egg yolks
500ml milk
salt flakes (large pinch of)

Salted Caramel

100g golden caster sugar
salt flakes (large pinch of)

Garnish

raspberries
viola flowers
baby mint
grated dark chocolate
leftover brownie

Method

> **Chef's Tip**
> We recommend making this the day before and freezing it fully. Bake just as you are ready to serve.

For The Brownies

Mix the butter, sugar, eggs, flour, cocoa powder and chocolate chunks in an electric mixer until the ingredients are thoroughly combined and the batter reaches a smooth and even consistency. Pour into a lined 18cm x 7cm square tin and bake at 180°C for 30 to 35 minutes. Cool, then divide into four. The brownie should mould very easily around the ball of ice cream.

For The Ice Cream

Use 100g of the sugar, add a pinch of salt and heat to make a caramel. Add this to the milk and remaining sugar. Heat and infuse. Whisk the eggs into a *sabayon*, then add the milk mixture and stir. Churn the ice cream mix in an ice cream maker. Alternatively, freeze the mixture, taking it out to stir every half hour, until it is completely set.

Scoop the ice cream into a ball shape and put it on a tooth pick. Mould the cooled chocolate brownie around the ice cream ball. You need four ice cream and brownie balls. Freeze for two hours. Remove tooth pick before baking.

For The Italian Meringue

Whisk the egg whites and cream of tartar until soft peaks form. Heat the sugar and water in a saucepan to 240°C until a soft ball stage is reached. Add slowly to the egg white mixture. Pipe the Italian meringue onto the ice cream filled chocolate brownie to make the outer layer of the Alaska and freeze once again for two hours.

To Serve

Bake the Alaska in the oven at 240°C for three minutes until golden. Place the Alaska in the centre of the plate. Put a scoop of the remaining ice cream to the side of the Alaska. Decorate with pieces of the left over brownie, grated chocolate, dots of salted caramel and mint leaves and flowers.

122
COLMANS

176 - 186 Ocean Road, South Shields, Tyne and Wear, NE33 2JQ

0191 456 1202
www.colmansfishandchips.com

Colmans of South Shields has become a landmark seafood restaurant and a North East institution. This family business was founded in 1926 with a culture of providing an excellent product combined with a first class service that continues to this day.

Richard and Frances Ord are the current 'stewards' of the Colman brand and they have, in recent years, added a level of sophistication and style to the business while never losing sight of the prime product - traditional fish and chips!

The Colmans team are also enthusiastic advocates of offering their customers a variety of local and sustainably sourced fish and sea foods. The daily landed, hand peeled langoustines, lightly battered and deep fried, is a product that could easily be served in any fine dining restaurant and should not be missed when you visit Colmans.

Locally caught and prepared on the premises, crab, lobster, squid and many other sustainable species from the North Sea are also available every day at Colmans. However traditional fish and chips remain the firm favourite. At Colmans, we believe we are blessed to be situated on the North East coast, where we firmly believe we have access to some of the world's finest fish and seafoods.

Our team provide an experience at Colmans that makes you want to return again and again. They look forward to seeing you!

Relish Restaurant Rewards
See page 003 for details.

At Colmans, we believe we are blessed to be situated on the North East coast, where we firmly believe we have access to some of the world's finest fish and seafoods.

QUEENIE SCALLOPS

SERVES 2

🍷 *Chablis*
(Burgundy, France)

Method

Preheat the oven to 180°C.

Start by clarifying the butter. To do this, melt the butter gently in a pan and scoop off any solids that form on the surface. Carefully ladle the clear and melted butter from the milky liquid, and keep it to one side until you need it.

Divide the scallops between the four shells or dishes. Add the chopped garlic to the *clarified butter* and pour a tablespoon of the garlic butter over each portion of scallops, followed by a squeeze of lemon. Lightly season with salt and pepper.

Sprinkle the Cheddar over the scallops, followed by the Gruyère and the breadcrumbs.

Keep in the fridge until you need them. Cook for eight minutes, on the top shelf of the oven, or until golden.

To Serve

Arrange as pictured.

Ingredients

24 queen scallops*
200g butter
3 cloves garlic (finely chopped)
lemon juice
200g medium Cheddar (grated)
100g Gruyère (grated)
2 tbsp breadcrumbs
salt and pepper

4 king scallop shells for serving, or 4 shallow dishes

*for all our recipes please use sustainable fish, MSC certified if possible

Garnish

chives
mixed salad leaves
lemon wedges
fresh grapefruit segments

CREAMY MUSSELS WITH SMOKY BACON & CIDER

SERVES 2

🍷 *Sauvignon Blanc
(New Zealand)*

Ingredients

Mussels

olive oil
6 rashers high-welfare smoked streaky bacon
(sliced 1cm thick)
1kg mussels (from sustainable sources - ask your
fishmonger, de-bearded and scrubbed clean)
1 clove garlic (peeled and finely sliced)
150ml good quality cider
2 tbsp fat free natural yoghurt
1 small bunch fresh tarragon (leaves picked and
roughly chopped)
1 small bunch fresh flat leaf parsley (leaves
picked and roughly chopped)

Toast

$^1/_2$ - 1 loaf good quality rustic bread or ciabatta
(sliced 2cm thick)
1 clove garlic (halved)
extra virgin olive oil

Method

For The Toast

Toast the bread on a screaming hot griddle, in the toaster,
or under a hot grill. When toasted, rub with the cut side of a
clove of garlic and drizzle lightly with extra virgin olive oil.

For The Mussels

Put a large pan on a high heat with a splash of olive oil.
Once hot, add the sliced bacon, stir and cook for a couple of
minutes, or until golden and crispy. Scoop the bacon out of the
pan, leaving the flavoured fat behind.

Check your mussels. If any of them are open just give them a
little tap and they should close - if they don't close, they are no
good to eat, so throw those ones away.

Add the mussels to the hot pan with the garlic, cider and a
good splash of olive oil. Cover with a lid and leave to steam for
three to four minutes, or until the mussels have opened and are
soft, juicy and delicious. Shake the pan occasionally.

When all of the mussels have opened, they're ready. Transfer to
a large platter, leaving the juices behind in the pan. If any of the
mussels have remained closed, throw away. Lay your toasts
around the edge of the platter.

To Serve

Stir the yoghurt into the pan then let it come to a boil and
bubble away for a couple of minutes. Add most of the herbs and
a little of the cooked bacon. Taste and season with pepper.
Give the pan a jiggle, then pour the sauce over the mussels.
Scatter over the remaining herbs and bacon, then put the
platter in the middle of the table and let everyone tuck in!

QUICK OMELETTE ARNOLD BENNETT

SERVES 2

🍷 *Albarino*
(Spain)

Method

Poach the haddock in the cream. This will only take a minute or two as being smoked haddock it is virtually cooked. Remove the haddock from the cream and break into large flakes. Set aside.

Melt the butter in a non-stick pan over a medium heat. Pour in the beaten, seasoned eggs and cook until they are dry around the edges, but still very moist in the middle. Remove from the heat.

To Serve

Sprinkle the omelette with the flaked haddock, and spoon over the poaching cream. Ensure the entire omelette and fish has a thin coating all over. Sprinkle over the grated parmesan and place under the hot grill. When brown and bubbling, sprinkle with chopped chives and transfer to a plate.

Serve with a leafy salad.

Ingredients

6 free range eggs (beaten and seasoned)
200g un-dyed smoked haddock
12 tbsp double cream
3 tbsp Parmesan (grated)
200g butter
salt and pepper

Garnish

chopped chives
mixed salad leaves

132
DABBAWAL

69-75 High Bridge, Newcastle upon Tyne, NE1 6BX
1 Brentwood Mews, Jesmond, NE2 3DG

High Bridge: 0191 232 5133
Jesmond: 0191 281 3434
www.dabbawal.com

Dabbawal has firmly positioned itself as the street food pioneer of the North East, introducing foodies to the many flavours of India's city streets with a trademark Dabbawal twist.

The craze for street food has taken a major hold since the first Dabbawal opened in Newcastle's High Bridge in 2011; introducing premium quality, street-inspired food served tapas-style in a cool, urban interior.

Regulars return time and again to enjoy the unique Dabbawal experience, savouring the fresh flavours of the street in a colourful, open kitchen venue - where a vibrant daytime vibes settle into chic, intimate evenings.

The hidden location of the second Dabbawal on Brentwood Mews, Jesmond, creates a magical serendipity to the bright, happening new restaurant, which opened summer 2013.

The Dabbawal experience is all about sharing and grazing; its signature street food snacks are tapas-style dishes and classic plates, taking diners on a journey of many different, unique flavours.

The express pre-theatre menu makes for a lively start to the evening and the fast-changing lunch menu features fresh, wholesome options and Newcastle's only roomali roti wraps.

Dabbawal takes the tastes of the street to a level you won't find anywhere else, served in a buzzing environment which has become the talk of the town. Taste the freshness!

Relish Restaurant Rewards
See page 003 for details.

Estd 2011

Dabbawal boasts an experienced crew including a dedicated team of skilled chefs and cocktail barmen. The chefs take regular trips to India and the continent for inspiration, ensuring their street food inspired menu remains fresh and authentic. The restaurant was nominated in the British Curry Awards for both best national newcomer and best restaurant in the North last year, testament to the quality and originality of the Dabbawal offering.

CHICKEN CHILLI FRY

SERVES 4

🍷 *Sauvignon Blanc Vidal Estate Marlborough (New Zealand)*

Method

Heat two tablespoons of oil in a pan. Add the curry leaves and mustard seeds and fry on a medium to high heat for one to two minutes. Leave to one side.

Cut the chicken into small strips, approximately 1cm x 3cm. Add to a pan with three tablespoons of oil and cook through. Once cooked, drain the chicken to get rid of any excess oil. Leave to stand for ten minutes.

In a separate pan, heat three tablespoons of oil and add the onions and peppers with a teaspoon of salt. Continue to stir until the onions begin to soften.

Now add the earlier prepared curry leaves and mustard seeds mixture to the onions and peppers and stir.

Follow by adding turmeric, chilli, paprika and black pepper and continue to stir until all the spices are mixed in well.

Finally, add fresh lemon juice and coconut milk powder and stir well.

Chef's Tip

To give the dish that professional look, fill a ramekin dish or tea cup full with the fry, pressing down to pack in. Place a plate on top and tip the ramekin or tea cup upside down and gently slide the dish off to create a clean, neat shape. Garnish with two chive sprigs.

To Serve

Serve as pictured and enjoy.

Ingredients

2 chicken breasts
2 medium sized white onions (chopped)
1 red pepper (cut into strips)
1 tsp chilli powder
1$\frac{1}{2}$ tsp paprika powder
$\frac{1}{2}$ tbsp turmeric powder
1tsp lemon juice
1tsp black pepper
2 tbsp coconut milk powder
5 - 6 curry leaves
2 tsp mustard seeds
8 tbsp cooking oil
salt (to taste)

Garnish

2 chive sprigs

LAMB BIRYANI

SERVES 4

Mr Smith Shiraz
(Australia)

Ingredients

450g lamb (diced into bite-sized pieces)

Marinade

2cm ginger (peeled and grated)
2 tsp ginger and garlic paste
1 tsp chilli powder
1 tsp turmeric
3 tsp garam masala
small handful mint (roughly chopped)
1 tsp black peppercorns (crushed)
1 stick cinnamon (broken in half)
125ml natural yoghurt
2 tbsp sunflower oil

Biryani

300g basmati rice
1 tsp cumin seeds
2 onions (sliced)
3 tomatoes (seeds removed and diced)
3 bay leaves

Vegetable Curry

2 white onions (sliced)
500g seasonal vegetables
$1/2$ tsp chilli powder
$1/2$ tsp Madras curry powder
salt (to taste)
400ml water
3 - 4 tbsp oil

Raita

300ml plain yoghurt
$1/4$ tsp cumin powder
$1/2$ cucumber (grated)
3 - 4 mint leaves (finely chopped)
$1/2$ tsp sugar
salt (to taste)

Garnish

100g crispy fried onions
coriander

Method

To Marinate The Lamb (Best prepared the day before)

Place all the ingredients of the marinade in a glass bowl and mix well. Add the lamb pieces and chill for at least two hours (or ideally overnight). Remove from the fridge one hour before cooking.

For The Biryani

Prepare the rice by soaking it for at least 30 minutes and rinsing well in a sieve until the water runs clear.

Add the oil to a large hot pan and fry the cumin seeds until they sizzle. When sizzling, add the onions and fry until soft and brown.

Pour in the lamb mix. Add the tomatoes and continue to cook on a high heat for five minutes, continually stirring, to make sure the spices are cooked through.

Turn the heat to low, cover and simmer for 25 minutes to ensure the lamb becomes tender.

Add the bay leaves and rice. Stir and cover again. Leave on a low heat for a further 20 minutes.

Turn off the heat and remove the lid. Stir once, then replace the lid.

Let it stand for ten minutes to ensure the rice is light and fluffy.

For The Vegetable Curry

Heat the oil in a pan on a medium heat. Add the onions and stir, allowing to soften. Add the chilli powder and curry powder and stir. Add a little water to avoid the onions burning. After two to three minutes, add your seasonal mix of vegetables and stir. Leave to cook for four to five minutes, then add water to create a sauce. Leave for 20 to 30 minutes on a low heat to allow the sauce to thicken, stirring occasionally. Season.

For The Raita

Pour the plain yoghurt into a medium-sized bowl. Follow by adding the cumin powder, grated cucumber, mint leaves and sugar. Finally, add salt to taste and mix well into a smooth paste.

To Serve

Garnish with fried onions and serve the dish as pictured with vegetable curry and raita.

GULAB JAMUN

SERVES 4

🍷 *Espresso Martini*
(After dinner)

Method

Mix the milk powder with the bicarbonate of soda, refined flour, green cardamom powder and a little water to make a soft dough.

Divide the dough into sixteen equal portions. Apply a little oil to the palms of your hands and shape the dough into round smooth balls, ensuring there are no cracks in the dough.

Prepare the sugar syrup in a pan by adding together the sugar with two cups of water and a pinch of saffron. Bring to a boil, then simmer for five minutes, making sure the syrup is clear and smooth.

Heat the oil in a kadai or wok. Add the balls and deepfry on a low heat until golden brown.

Drain the excess oil, then soak in the sugar syrup for at least 15 to 20 minutes before serving.

Chef's Tip

The temperature of the oil should be low to ensure the jamuns cook through.

Ingredients

1 cup milk powder
1/4 tsp bicarbonate of soda
3 tbsp refined flour
1/4 tsp green cardamom powder
2 cups sugar
2 cups water
saffron (pinch of)
oil (to deepfry)

Garnish

1 strawberry (sliced)
1 tsp raspberry compote
1 scoop of vanilla ice cream
1 mint sprig

142
DAVID KENNEDY AT VALLUM

Military Road, East Wallhouses, Newcastle upon Tyne, NE18 0LL

01434 672 406
www.vallumfarm.co.uk

For David Kennedy, Vallum is a chef's dream, as it is nestled amongst a hub of artisan producers in the heart of Northumberland.

On-site we have Ken, Tracy and Mark who have created the Vallum kitchen garden, which has changed my approach to food. I now choose the vegetables first, then the protein to go alongside. The lovely, lightly smoked meat and locally landed fish by Bernard from Bywell smokery is always on the menus in some form and sells out every week in the shop. We use produce from Vicky Moffitt's award-winning ice cream parlour, and now cheese parlour, and are delighted to have baker Murray Rhine producing amazing bread and pâtisserie again for the shop.

Their food, grow-your-own produce masterclasses in the fields, the newly arrived chef's pod and amazing bespoke shepherd's hut in the Vallum kitchen garden, all offer something unique to the site.

Relish Restaurant Rewards
See page 003 for details.

Our aim and ethos is governed by the array of products we use from the Vallum site. This creates a stunning and unique set up in the North East. Eventually 80% of the products in our shop will be produced in the Vallum postcode.

OVERNIGHT BRAISED LOCAL RABBIT, GARNISHED FROM THE VALLUM KITCHEN GARDEN

SERVES 4

🍷 *Viognier*
(France)

Ingredients

Rabbit

2 rabbit legs
50g grey sea salt
2 bay leaves
2 sprigs thyme (chopped)
1 clove garlic (finely sliced)
1 tsp white peppercorns (crushed)
1kg duck fat

Dressing

100ml rapeseed oil
25ml sherry vinegar
salt and pepper

Vegetables

handful each of:
radish
fennel
carrots
pea shoots
spring onions
beetroot leaves

Method

For The Rabbit (Prepare the day before)

Liberally cover the rabbit legs with the salt, bay leaves, thyme, garlic and peppercorns. Leave for 24 hours.

The next day, rinse off the legs, pat dry and place in an ovenproof dish, cover with duck fat and cook in the oven at 140°C for three hours. Once cooked, allow to cool in the fat.

For The Vegetables

Wash and scrub the soil from the vegetables and set aside.

For The Dressing

Make the dressing by whisking the oil, vinegar and seasoning together.

To Serve

When the rabbit is cool enough to handle, drain and flake the rabbit, being careful to remove all the bones. Gently break down the rabbit into flakes and add a little of the duck fat to moisten.

Place the rabbit in the middle of the plate and arrange the vegetables around it. Drizzle with the dressing.

SLOW COOKED HAKE, SPRING VEGETABLE BROTH, SMOKED MACKEREL CROQUETTE

SERVES 4

🍷 *Oaked white Rioja*
(Spain)

Ingredients

Fish
4 fillets hake
knob of butter
lemon juice (squeeze of)

Spring Vegetable Broth
4 salad onions
4 radishes
4 turnips
4 English asparagus spears (peeled)
8 mint leaves
handful broad beans and peas
100g unsalted butter
20ml vegetable oil
$^{1}/_{2}$ lemon (juice of)
salt and pepper

Croquette
300g mashed potato
100g smoked mackerel (flaked)
20g parsley (chopped)
1 orange (zest of)
100g breadcrumbs
20g plain flour
1 egg (beaten)

Method

For The Croquette

Mix together the potato, mackerel, parsley, orange and seasoning. Place into a piping bag and pipe the mixture, each about 5cm long, onto the tray. Pop into the fridge to firm up. *Pane* once firm. Use the egg, flour and double breadcrumb. Return to the fridge until ready to use.

For The Fish

Bring a non-stick pan to a high heat, add a splash of oil and place the fillets skin side down. Season, then place in a hot oven at 180°C for about four minutes.

For The Spring Vegetable Broth

Place the onions and radish in a pan and just cover with water. Bring to a boil then add the butter gradually. Season, add the remaining vegetables and mint and cook for one minute. Add a squeeze of lemon juice. Set aside.

To Finish

Add a touch of butter to the fish and leave to rest in the pan for two minutes. Add a squeeze of lemon and turn the fish over in the pan.

Deep fry the croquette at 170°C for four minutes.

To Serve

Place the broth in a shallow bowl. Arrange the fish and croquette on top.

CHERRY TART, CREME FRAICHE & PISTACHIOS

SERVES 4

🍷 *Champagne*
(France)

Method

For The Cherries

Place the cherries, sugar and just enough water to cover in a pan. Bring to a simmer and cook for five minutes until soft.

For The Pastry Case

Roll and cut out the pastry to your desired shapes. Brush with the egg yolk and sprinkle with the brown sugar. Bake in a hot oven at 180°C for nine minutes. Allow to cool.

Alternatively, you can use ready-made pastry cases.

For The Isomalt Dome

Warm the Isomalt in a pan and spoon into small rings on a greaseproofed baking sheet or baking mat. Whilst still hot, place a metal ring in the rings of isomalt and slowly pull the ring up to form a dome shape.

To Serve

Place the pastry case on a plate. Pile the softened cherries on top, then some of the remaining fresh cherries. Place the isomalt dome on top of the cherries. Add a spoonful of crème fraîche alongside and sprinkle with pistachios.

Ingredients

Cherries
400g cherries (stoned)
30g sugar

Pastry Case
400g shortcrust pastry (or puff pastry)
20g brown sugar
30ml egg yolk

Isomalt Dome
300g Isomalt

Garnish
400g cherries (stoned)
100g pistachios (nibbed)
200g crème fraîche

152
THE DUKE OF WELLINGTON INN

Newton, Nr Corbridge, Northumberland, NE43 7UL

01661 844 446
www.thedukeofwellingtoninn.co.uk

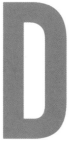

Despite a reputation that travels far beyond the regional boundaries, and throngs of guests who travel from far and wide to sample its outstanding cuisine, commitment to the community and the North East region remains the priority for The Duke of Wellington Inn.

The venue, which boasts spectacular views from its setting in the Tyne Valley, prides itself on being at the heart of its locality. From acting as the local pub and meeting place for the small Northumberland community in which it is based, to sourcing suppliers and ingredients locally for its restaurant, the local focus of The Duke of Wellington is clear.

While also a focal point for tourism in Northumberland, with its five star accommodation and famous quality of food, the 'Wellie' - as it is affectionately known - translates its community focus into being able to offer the most informal and welcoming ambience and a true 'home from home' environment for guests, who travel from across the country to visit.

Based in the village of Newton, near Corbridge, the Wellie prides itself on its award-winning food. Using locally sourced, seasonal ingredients, head chef, Gabor Pusztai and his team produce exceptional British cuisine and offer a menu packed with traditional hearty dishes. Staying true to its informality, dishes at the Wellie include staple favourites like its famous fish and chips, although there are few choices on the menu which may be regarded as unusual. But the outstanding quality of food is what truly makes the venue's reputation and has won the Wellie a legion of fans - not to mention accolades - throughout the culinary world.

Quality runs throughout the operation at the Wellie and its accommodation is rated as being of the highest standard. Having recently undergone an extensive refurbishment, its seven guest rooms all boast luxury, but with a distinctly Northumbrian feel. Throughout the renovation, it remained imperative that the new design, although more modern, must not stray from the traditional and homely feel for which the Wellie has become known and loved. While the existing oak and stone has remained, it is now accompanied by modern colours, furniture and fabrics, adding a 21st Century touch to the historic coaching inn.

Relish Restaurant Rewards
See page 003 for details.

Head chef, Gabor Pusztai, North East Chef of the Year 2013, and his team are passionate supporters of local produce. Northumberland certainly provides a stunning variety of vegetables, meat and fish. With an ample supply of fields, woods, rivers and sea shore, foraging also has a part to play in sourcing ingredients. Local fisherman and hunters provide a supply of fresh fish and game.

FOIE GRAS WITH BEETROOT, CHERRY & VANILLA

SERVES 6

🍷 *Château Raymond Lafon, Sauternes
(Bordeaux, France)*

Ingredients

Beetroot

3 large beetroots
200g caster sugar
375ml red wine
200ml red wine vinegar
200ml water
4 bay leaves
4 sprigs thyme
70g salt
10 black peppercorns

Cherry Vanilla Purée

500g cherries
1ltr beetroot liquor
1 vanilla pod (scraped)
salt (to taste)
sugar (to taste)

Foie Gras

1 lobe fresh foie gras
50ml Cognac
50ml port
20g pink salt

Baby Shallots

4 shallots
250ml beetroot liquor

Garnish

pea shoots
beetroot cress

Method

For The Beetroot

Bring all ingredients to a boil, apart from the beetroot. Peel the beetroot and add to the pan. Gently simmer in a covered pan until the beetroot is cooked through. Allow the liquor to cool. Strain the beetroot and retain the liquor for the purée and shallots.

For The Cherry Vanilla Purée

Simmer the cherries in the beetroot liquor for 30 minutes until most of the liquor is absorbed and the cherries are soft. Purée the beetroot and cherries with some of the beetroot liquor to achieve a silky smooth texture. Season to taste with salt, sugar and the vanilla seeds.

For The Foie Gras (Prepare the day before)

Cure the foie gras with Cognac, port and pink salt at room temperature for three hours until soft and supple. Rinse under cold running water. Ensure that the foie gras has no veins or arteries. Place in the fridge for 30 minutes. Stretch out a length of clingfilm over the work surface and place the foie gras in the middle. Roll into a tight *ballotine*. Place the *ballotine* of foie gras into a container of iced water and leave for one hour. Transfer to the fridge to cool overnight.

For The Baby Shallots

Blanch the shallots whole, then cut in half. Place flat side down in a tray. Fill the tray with beetroot liquor until half way up the shallots. Leave to pickle, so that the top half stays white.

To Serve

Plate as pictured and garnish with pea shoots and beetroot cress.

PIG'S TROTTER BALLOTINE WITH TARRAGON PEA PUREE, CRACKLING CRUMBLE & VALLUM FARM VEGETABLES

SERVES 3

🍷 *Sauska Tokaj (Dry White) (Hungary)*

Ingredients

Tarragon Pea Purée

25g butter
3 large shallots
2 cloves garlic
50g frozen garden peas
1 sprig thyme
600ml milk
ground white pepper
salt

Pig Trotter Ballotine And Crackling Crumble

6 - 8 pig trotters (and skin for crackling)
5 cloves garlic
2 baby carrots
1 baby leek
2 sticks celery (sliced)
2ltrs chicken stock
2 baby white onions
3 bay leaves
salt and ground white pepper
parsley
2 sprigs thyme (picked)
1 shallot (chopped)
150ml white port

1 tsp duck fat (with herbs and garlic)

Garnish

Vallum Farm vegetables
pork jus
girolle mushrooms
fresh peas (*blanched*, refreshed and warmed)

Method

For The Tarragon Pea Purée

Melt the butter in a pan. Add the garlic and chopped shallots and cook for three to five minutes until soft, but not coloured. Add the peas and the tarragon and cook for a further four to five minutes. Drain the peas and blend in a food processor with the tarragon. Slowly add the milk until smooth. Pass through a fine sieve.

For The Pig Trotter Ballotine (Prepare the day before)

Place the trotters, pork skin, garlic, carrots, leek, celery, onions, chicken stock and bay leaves in a large pot and cook slowly for six hours. Once cooked, separate the meat and fat of the trotters from the bones. Put the trotter meat and some of the fat into a bowl and season with salt, ground white pepper, parsley and some of the thyme. Place the port, shallot and the rest of the thyme in a pan and reduce until the liquor has almost disappeared. Add this to the trotter mixture. Stretch out a length of clingfilm over the work surface and place the trotter mixture in the middle. Roll the mixture in the clingfilm into a *ballotine* shape and place in the fridge to cool overnight.

For The Crackling Crumble (Prepare two days before)

Place the cooked pork skin on a rack for two days to dehydrate. Deepfry the skin until puffed up. Chop up with a knife to crumble.

To Serve

Slice the *ballotine* into six equal portions (leaving the clingfilm on). Seal on all sides in the duck fat, herbs and garlic. Cook in a moderately hot oven for six to seven minutes. Once cooked, remove the clingfilm. Garnish with the pea purée, Vallum Farm vegetables, crackling crumble, pork jus and girolle mushrooms.

MOLTEN CHOCOLATE CAKE WITH ROASTED COFFEE ICE CREAM, CHOCOLATE SHORTBREAD SHELL & CHOCOLATE SAUCE

SERVES 6

Tawny Port
(Portugal)

Ingredients

Chocolate Shortbread Shells

250g plain flour
120g butter
8g cocoa powder
4g salt
50g egg yolk
100g granulated sugar
250g dark chocolate (70% cocoa)

Molten Chocolate Cake

250g butter
200g dark chocolate
100g egg yolk, 150g egg white
100g caster sugar, 25g icing sugar
25g plain flour

Roasted Coffee Ice Cream

700ml milk
20g ground coffee
10g coffee extract, 15g instant coffee
50g glucose
400g evaporated milk
3 egg yolks

Chocolate Sauce

50ml milk, 50ml cream
70g glucose
400g dark chocolate
50g dark chocolate (70% cocoa)

Vanilla Emulsion

400ml milk
600ml whipped cream
1 vanilla pod (seeds)
140g caster sugar
4 sheets gelatine, 2 gas guns

Garnish

crumbled chocolate
honeycomb

Method

For The Chocolate Shortbread Shells

Mix together all of the ingredients, except the chocolate. Allow the dough to rest for two hours in the fridge. Once chilled, roll out to 2 to 3mm thick and line silicone egg shell moulds. Fill the pastry with clingfilm covered dry beans or baking beans. Cook for ten to 12 minutes at 180°C.

Melt the chocolate in a *bain-marie* and pour into silicone egg shell moulds. Leave for half an hour and pour out the excess chocolate. Put the shells in the fridge to set.

For The Molten Chocolate Cake

Melt the butter and chocolate in a *bain-marie*. Beat the egg yolk and sugar together until pale. Beat the egg white and icing sugar together. Fold all three components together and sieve in the flour and mix. Pour about 16g of chocolate mixture into each mould and refrigerate for 30 minutes. Preheat oven to 180°C and bake for five minutes.

For The Roasted Coffee Ice Cream

Boil all the ingredients together at 75°C and cool down on ice. Pour the mixture into an ice cream maker and churn. Keep in a freezer until ready to serve.

For The Chocolate Sauce

Melt all ingredients over a *bain-marie* and leave to one side.

For The Vanilla Emulsion

Soak the gelatine in water. Boil all the other ingredients together. Squeeze the gelatine into the mixture and transfer to the gun. Place in the fridge until ready to use.

To Serve

Position the shortbread shell onto a bed of crumbled chocolate. Crumble the molten chocolate cake into the shell and top with the vanilla emulsion and roasted coffee ice cream. Cover with the dark chocolate shell and garnish with honeycomb. Serve with warm chocolate sauce.

162
EL GATO NEGRO TAPAS

1 Oldham Road, Ripponden, Sowerby Bridge, West Yorkshire, HX6 4DN

01422 823 070
www.elgatonegrotapas.com

The surrounding countryside is more windswept than sun-baked, and the buildings are traditional sandstone, darkened by time, not the dazzling white buildings of Andalucía. Walk down a steep and picturesque cobbled street and you'll reach a humped back bridge, beyond which nestles a small church spire. This is a classic Yorkshire town, but also home to a very successful tapas restaurant, sandwiched between a row of small local shops. A striking black cat stares out from the billboard above the door of El Gato Negro Tapas, formerly The Junction pub, in the small town of Ripponden. It's nowhere near Las Ramblas, but El Gato is bristling with the inspiration and influence of Barcelona.

We opened back in 2005 with the aim of bringing some of the magic of modern Spanish cooking to Yorkshire and that remains our passion to this day.

Our dishes are about combining the best ingredients, be they Spanish or locally sourced, with modern techniques which are rooted in tradition.

The result for me is all about creating bold, distinctive cuisine complemented by a range of great and interesting Spanish wines and sharing that experience in a relaxed, friendly environment. Here we offer a small selection of some of our award-winning dishes.

We look forward to welcoming you soon

Salud!

Simon

Relish Restaurant Rewards
See page 003 for details.

EL GATO NEGRO TAPAS

0 1422 823 070

Our dishes are about combining the best ingredients, be they Spanish or locally sourced, with modern techniques which are rooted in tradition.

HAND PICKED WHITE CRABMEAT, AVOCADO PUREE & GAZPACHO

SERVES 4

Louro, Godello
(Spain)

Ingredients

Crab

200g pure white crab claw meat
2 eggs (hardboiled and finely grated)
1 medium sized banana shallot (finely diced)
Tabasco (to taste)
1 lemon (squeeze of)
100g aioli (see recipe below) or good quality mayonnaise
salt and pepper

Avocado Purée

1 Hass avocado
$1/2$ tsp ascorbic acid
1 lemon (squeeze of)
salt and pepper

Aioli

4 egg yolks
50ml white wine vinegar
25g Dijon mustard
6 cloves garlic (crushed to a paste)
1.3ltrs vegetable oil
salt and pepper

Gazpacho

150g tomato pulp
200ml concentrated tomato juice
100ml sherry vinegar
1 cucumber (peeled and roughly chopped, with seeds left in)
1 sweet red pepper
1 red onion (roughly chopped)
1 bunch spring onions (roughly chopped)
2 bulbs garlic (roughly chopped)
300ml good olive oil

Method

For The Aioli

Mix together the egg yolks, white wine vinegar and mustard to make a paste. Add the crushed garlic. Slowly whisk in the oil until the aioli reaches a smooth consistency. Season to taste with salt and pepper. Refrigerate until needed.

For The Crab

Pick through the crabmeat and discard any shell. Add the grated eggs, shallot, some of the lemon juice and Tabasco. Season with salt and pepper. Add the aioli or mayonnaise, check seasoning and set aside.

For The Avocado Purée

Peel and cut the avocado into chunks. Blend with the ascorbic acid, a little lemon juice and salt and pepper to taste. Pass through a fine sieve and set aside.

For The Gazpacho

Put all ingredients into a liquidiser and blend to a smooth consistency. Pass through a sieve and refrigerate.

To Serve

Take a small glass jar or Martini glass. Start by putting the avocado purée into the bottom of the glass. Give it a little tap to level out the avocado, then top with the crab mixture. Level with a teaspoon, leaving a gap one inch from the top and refrigerate. When ready to serve, finish with gazpacho, a little olive oil, rock salt and pepper.

ALEJANDRO CHORIZO WITH PIQUILLO PEPPER & AIOLI

SERVES 4

🍷 *Casal de Paula Ribeiro Tinto Galicia (Spain)*

Ingredients

Chorizo

500g Alejandro Chorizo hoops
200ml good quality chicken stock
100ml dry cider
50g aioli (see previous recipe)

Piquillo Pepper Purée

100g Piquillo Peppers
25ml good quality tomato juice

Garnish

25ml balsamic vinegar (preferably Fresh Olive Company balsamic)
parsley oil
La Chinata smoked paprika
chives

Method

For The Chorizo

Place the chorizo hoops into a sous-vide bag and cook in a water bath at 75°C for six hours. Remove and plunge into ice water until the product has totally cooled down. Refrigerate.

Alternatively, poach the chorizo in chicken stock with a little cider. This could be done on a pilot light overnight. Make sure to totally cover the chorizo and cover with tinfoil. Follow the same cooling process as with the sous-vide method.

For The Piquillo Pepper Purée

To make the Piquillo pepper purée, blend the peppers with the tomato juice in a liquidiser to reach a smooth consistency. Pass through a fine sieve and put into a plastic squeezy bottle. Set aside.

To Finish And Serve

Cut the Alejandro chorizo into 20 even sized barrels pieces. Re-vacuum pack the chorizo, five pieces per portion, and put back in the water bath for approximately 30 minutes at 75°C, or alternatively, re-heat in some chicken stock for approximately 30 to 45 minutes over a low heat.

Mix together the 200ml of chicken stock with 100ml of cider. Reduce by half, then add the heated chorizo and reduce until all the sausage has an even glaze (there should be no liquid left in the pan). Keep warm.

Ideally, take an oblong plate, add a blob of the Piquillo pepper purée and swipe across the plate. Dress the plate with balsamic and a little parsley oil. Arrange the five barrel pieces of chorizo side by side and top with aioli.

VALRHONA CHOCOLATE DELICE

SERVES 4

🍷 *Fernando De Castilla Pedro Ximenez Antique
(Spain)*

Ingredients

Chocolate Mousse

220ml full fat milk
3 egg yolks
75g sugar
150g dark Valrhona chocolate (80% cocoa)
300ml double cream (whipped)
3 leaves gelatine

Chocolate Sponge

2 whole eggs
50g caster sugar
25g plain flour
25g cocoa powder

Chocolate Mirror Topping

125g caster sugar
125g water
40g cocoa powder
250g double cream
1 Mars Bar (chopped)
1 leaf gelatine (soaked in cold water)

Garnish

raspberries
Grand Marnier
mint leaves

15cm square mould

Method

For The Mousse

Soften the gelatine in cold water and set aside. Bring the milk to a boil, cream together the egg yolks and sugar then add the hot milk. Cook the mixture in a stainless steel bowl over a pan of boiling water until the mixture is light and fluffy (ribbon stage). Remove from the heat and keep whisking, add the gelatine (after squeezing out all the excess water). Add the chocolate and continue to whisk until all the chocolate has melted. Once the mixture has cooled, fold in the whipped cream to achieve a mousse consistency.

For The Sponge

With an electric whisk, beat the two eggs with the sugar until the mixture has doubled in size. Fold in the flour and cocoa powder. Spread onto baking parchment and cook in a fan assisted oven at 180°C for approximately five to six minutes, or until the sponge springs back. Set aside.

For The Topping

In a saucepan, bring all the ingredients, except the cream, to a boil. Add the cream, bring back to a boil and simmer for approximately five minutes or until the Mars Bar has completely dissolved. Pass through a sieve and add the gelatine. Set aside.

To Serve

Line a 15cm square mould with the chocolate sponge. Sprinkle with a little Grand Marnier to wet the sponge. Pour the chocolate mousse mixture over the sponge, almost to the top. Refrigerate until the mousse sets. When set, pour over the chocolate mirror glaze so that it covers all of the mousse. Return to the fridge for the glaze to set (this will take approximately 30 minutes). De-mould the délice with a blow torch and cut into four even pieces and plate.

> **Chef's Tip**
>
> At El Gato we brush the plate with a little of the mirror topping for decoration and the délice is topped with three resh raspberries filled with raspberry sauce, and garnished with a sprig of mint.

172
ERIC'S

73-75 Lidget Street, Lindley, Huddersfield, West Yorkshire, HD3 3JP

01484 646 416
www.ericsrestaurant.co.uk

Our friendly neighbourhood restaurant is achieving a popular following from customers far and wide.

Before opening Eric's in 2010, our accomplished and enthusiastic head chef and proprietor, Eric Paxman, worked around the world and trained under the best. Eric developed his craft working in London under Marco Pierre White at L'escargot, learning from Marco's fine and classical style. In Sydney, Australia, Eric worked under BBC1's Saturday Kitchen chef, Bill Grainger, for his three restaurants. Bill mentored Eric on creating good food with a modern twist and has been a huge influence for Eric's restaurant.

At Eric's we take the best aspects from our head chef's two previous mentors and reflect these in a personable and relaxed style, exuding an air of informality our customers love. Our exciting seasonal menus are crafted with flair and imagination, with emphasis on fine ingredients, which are sourced locally whenever possible.

Our comfortable, atmospheric restaurant is presented with as much attention to detail as the food. We are pleased to exhibit work by Yorkshire artists in the restaurant, adding interest and ambiance to the setting. Our bar area is the perfect place for pre-dinner drinks and cocktails, whilst our modern, comfortable surroundings are the perfect backdrop for experiencing Eric's passion for food and Yorkshire values.

Relish Restaurant Rewards
See page 003 for details.

We are very proud that our restaurant is widely talked about; ever popular amongst a growing numbers of customers and in restaurant reviews. We're listed in the Good Food Guide and are delighted to have gone on to be the current Good Food Guide's Regional Restaurant of the Year for the North East, as voted for by its readers.

CRISPY DUCK EGG, YORKSHIRE ASPARAGUS, CURED DUCK HAM, COLD PRESSED RAPESEED OIL & ENGLISH MUSTARD

SERVES 4

🍷 *'Fossili' Gavi del Comune di Gavi, San Silvestro (Italy)*

Ingredients

Crispy Duck Egg
4 large duck eggs
150g Panko breadcrumbs
1 egg (beaten)
100g plain flour (seasoned)

Mayonnaise
3 egg yolks
100ml white wine vinegar
50g English mustard
500ml cold pressed rapeseed oil

Asparagus
1/2 bunch Yorkshire asparagus (lightly peeled)
knob of butter (melted)

Garnish
cured duck ham (sliced)
mixed salad leaves
fresh peas (enough to serve)

Method

For The Crispy Duck Egg
Submerge the duck eggs in boiling water for seven minutes. Now carefully transfer the egg into iced water and leave to cool for five minutes. When cool, peel the egg (see chef's tip).

Get a bowl each for the flour, beaten egg and Panko breadcrumbs. Roll the duck egg in flour and coat evenly all over. Now transfer it to the beaten egg and again aim for an even coating. Next to the Panko breadcrumbs, rolling the duck egg for its final even coating.

> **Chef's Tip**
> To peel the duck egg, tap and roll it on a hard surface so that it cracks all over. Peel the whole shell off in one from the large end.

For The Mayonnaise
Blitz the three egg yolks, white wine vinegar and English mustard in a food processor (or hand blender) for one minute at high speed. When all the ingredients are incorporated and whilst still mixing slowly, start adding the cold pressed rapeseed oil in a very fine stream, until completely blended. Add water to desired consistency and season.

For The Asparagus
Submerge the asparagus in a pan of salted boiling water and boil until al dente (five to seven minutes). Drain and toss in melted butter for a nice glossy finish.

To Serve
Pipe the mayonnaise onto a platter. Arrange the duck ham and leaves so they stand tall and place the asparagus and peas around the mayonnaise. Slightly slice the bottom of the duck egg to help it stand up and slice the top so you can see the egg yolk inside. Carefully place the duck egg on top of salad.

PANFRIED SCARBOROUGH WOOF WITH SAUTEED SAMPHIRE GRASS, CHARGRILLED JERSEY ROYALS, AVOCADO MAYONNAISE, BRAISED RED PEPPERS & WILD GARLIC PESTO

SERVES 4

🍷 *Rabl Gruner Veltliner 'Spiegel'*
(Austria)

Ingredients

1kg prepared Scarborough Woof fillet
150g pancetta lardons

Vegetables

500g Jersey Royals (washed)
500g fresh samphire grass
6 red peppers
oil and butter (for frying)

Avocado Mayonnaise

3 ripe avocados
3 lemons (juiced and grated zest)
2 egg yolks
salt and pepper
500ml vegetable oil

Wild Garlic Pesto

250g wild garlic
20g pine nuts (toasted)
20g Parmesan (grated)
100ml olive oil
salt and pepper (to taste)

Garnish

purple shiso

Method

For The Vegetables

Firstly shallow fry the peppers in a frying pan until very dark brown in colour. Remove from the pan, place in an airtight container and leave to cool. When cool, peel off the dark skin and remove any stalks and seeds. Thinly slice the red flesh and place in the fridge until needed.

Cook the Jersey Royals in a pan of salted, boiling water and refresh in cold water. Slice in half when cooked.

To Prepare The Fish

Pull out any bones from the fish. Cut into four 225g portions and place back in t.he fridge.

> **Chef's Tip**
> If you can't find Scarborough Woof, this may be alternatively known by some fishmongers as Scotch halibut.

For The Mayonnaise

Remove the skin and stone from the avocados. Place the flesh in a blender along with the juice and zest of the lemons, egg yolks, salt and pepper. Blitz for four minutes and then slowly add the oil until it thickens. Check for seasoning and chill.

For The Pesto

Place all the ingredients into a blender and blitz to a smooth green purée.

For The Samphire

Wash the samphire grass in cold water then dry it well. Bring a pan of water to a boil and place the samphire in. Cook for four minutes. Drain and set to one side.

To Serve

Fry the fish on a medium heat until golden brown and firm to touch. Chargrill the Jersey Royals on a griddle. Fry the pancetta until crispy and add the peppers, potatoes and the samphire grass to the pan for two and three minutes. Check for seasoning.

Arrange the peppers, pancetta, potatoes and samphire centrally on a plate with the fish placed carefully on top. Add avocado mayonnaise to the side, drizzle with the pesto and garnish with shiso.

LEMON PARFAIT, ITALIAN MERINGUE & FRESH RASPBERRIES

SERVES 4

Grand Constance, Groot Constantia (South Africa)

Ingredients

Meringue
5 egg whites
250g caster sugar

Parfait
3 eggs
120g caster sugar
75ml lemon juice
100ml whipping cream
icing sugar (for dusting)

Garnish
1 punnet fresh raspberries
fresh mint
100g shortbread biscuits (blitzed)

4 metal moulds or rings, 8cm diameter

Method

For The Italian Meringue

Preheat the oven to 90°C. Whisk together the egg whites and caster sugar until they are a ribbon consistency and then place into a piping bag, saving two tablespoons of the mixture to chill separately. Line a tray with baking parchment (see chef's tip) and pipe out little meringues (about the size of raspberries) with even spacing. Bake until the meringues are nice and crisp, for approximately one hour.

> **Chef's Tip**
>
> To keep the baking parchment flat when making meringues, place a dot of meringue mixture onto each corner of the baking tray and stick the corners of the parchment to the dots.

For The Lemon Parfait

Preheat the oven to 120°C. Whisk the eggs and sugar together in a bowl.

In a pan, bring the cream and lemon juice to a boil. Pour this over the egg mixture and whisk until the sugar has completely dissolved. Pass the mixture through a fine sieve to get rid of any lumps. Next, line the bottom of four metal rings with clingfilm to form moulds (sticking the clingfilm to the outside of the ring). Pour the lemon mixture into the rings and fill three quarters full. Place these moulds into a tray and fill the tray a quarter full with warm water. The tray goes into the oven until the mix is just set with a slight wobble. Chill for one hour and then carefully turn out of the rings.

To Serve

Dust the lemon parfait with sieved icing sugar and glaze with a blow torch. Using the excess meringue mixture from the fridge, swipe some onto the plate and glaze also with a blow torch. Place the lemon parfait to one side and a line of shortbread biscuit crumbs to the other side of the meringue. On this, arrange raspberries and meringues, alternating between the two and garnish with fresh mint leaves.

THE FEATHERS INN

Hedley on the Hill, Stocksfield, Northumberland, NE43 7SW

01661 843 607
www.thefeathers.net

The Feathers Inn is an attractive 200-year-old traditional stone-built pub, high above the Tyne Valley, enjoying Northumbrian countryside views. The pub has always been a place of refreshment on the old road between Hadrian's Wall and the Derwent Valley. The Inn exudes character everywhere you look. Both bar areas have an old fashioned, homely feel with real fires, while tankards hang from exposed beams. The menu at The Feathers embraces the flavours of regional cookery and British classics. Rhian Cradock works to create these dishes with passion, incorporating the finest produce from the North East. Serving the finest local cask ales, ciders and carefully selected wines, customers travel considerable distances to reach this quiet, hilltop village and enjoy it's superb hospitality.

As the heart of the village and community life in Hedley, we host an active Leek Club, monthly Northumbrian folk music gatherings and regular special events such as farmers markets, wine nights, whisky tasting evenings, foraging events and an Easter beer and food festival.

The quality of the product is at the very heart of everything we do. We believe animal welfare is an essential aspect of ensuring quality, so we only work with farmers who put the welfare of their animals first and show care and attention to their needs.

The daily changing menu reflects our small-scale artisan producers and suppliers, and includes homemade black pudding and game from local estates. Rhian works closely with farmers and producers to select and showcase local produce, developing dishes that bring out the best of these products for our customers to enjoy.

Relish Restaurant Rewards
See page 003 for details.

It is our aim to serve the very best food and ale in a relaxed, informal and thoroughly professionally-run environment. "Cracking community local and top dining destination." David Hancock, editor of Sawday's.

Our awards include Local, Seasonal and Organic Produce Award 2013 and 2014, Pubs and Inns of England and Wales, Northumbria Dining Pub of the Year 2008, 2009, 2010, 2011 and 2013, Great British Pub of the Year 2011, Great British Gastro-pub of the Year 2011 and RSPCA Pub and Restaurant Award winner 2010 and 2011.

ENGLISH ASPARAGUS ON TOAST WITH ST GEORGE'S MUSHROOMS

SERVES 4

Leventhorpe Seyval Blanc
(Yorkshire, United Kingdom)

Method

Preheat the grill to high and toast the brioche. Keep warm in a low oven.

For The Asparagus

Have a large pan of boiling salted water ready. Trim the asparagus by snapping it at its natural breaking point and peeling it if it is larger than a pencil. Put the asparagus into the boiling water, it should take no more than two to three minutes - just time to cook the mushrooms.

For The Mushrooms

Heat a large frying pan. Put the butter in the frying pan and allow it to heat and colour slightly. Add the mushrooms and cook until they have released some moisture. Add the garlic, shallot, parsley, squeeze of lemon juice and seasoning.

To Serve

Pile the mushrooms on the brioche. Top with the asparagus, garnish with watercress and serve immediately.

Ingredients

16 spears English asparagus (4 per person)
4 slices brioche (sliced 2cm thick)

Mushrooms

200g St George's mushrooms or small button mushrooms (brushed and trimmed)
1 shallot (finely diced)
1 clove garlic (puréed)
lemon (squeeze of)
40g parsley leaves (washed and chopped)
50g unsalted butter
salt and pepper

Garnish

watercress

HEDLEY ROE DEER LOIN BAKED IN PASTRY WITH CHICKEN LIVER PATE & FIELD MUSHROOMS & SPRING VEGETABLES

SERVES 4

🍷 *Chateau Musar 2005, Gaston Hochar (Lebanon)*

Ingredients

Roe Deer Loin In Pastry

4 x 130g portions Roe deer loin
400g puff pastry (rolled 4mm thick, divided into 4 squares of approximately 15cm)
200g chicken liver pâté (or any other pâté of choice, cut into 4 x 25g slices)
200g field mushrooms
4 sprigs thyme (picked and chopped)
1 clove garlic (very finely chopped)
50ml olive oil
salt and pepper
1 egg yolk (whisked with 1 tsp water)

Red Wine, Port And Redcurrant Jelly Sauce

250g Roe deer bones and trimmings (roasted)
250ml red wine
100ml port
25g redcurrant jelly
500ml roasted chicken stock
water (to cover)
1 sprig rosemary
1 sprig thyme
$^1/_2$ bay leaf
1 clove garlic (peeled and bashed)
$^1/_2$ leek (washed and chopped)
1 carrot (peeled and cut into 2.5cm pieces)
2 stalks parsley
$^1/_2$ onion (diced into 2.5cm pieces)

To Serve

a selection of seasonal vegetables

Method

For The Roe Deer Loin in Pastry

Mix together the thyme, garlic and olive oil. Liberally drizzle over the mushrooms on a baking tray. Season and cook in a hot oven for 20 minutes. Remove when soft and cooked, with their juices leaking out. Chop finely, then dry the minced mushrooms in a pan, on a low heat, until all the liquid has evaporated.

Place onto a tray and leave to cool.

> **Chef's Tip**
> I prefer to use Roe deer venison which is available in our local area. The recipe can be used with any sort of venison such as Red deer or Fallow deer.

For The Loin

Season the loin portions and seal in a hot pan, so the meat caramelises. Set aside and rest.

To Assemble

Lay the rolled puff pastry out on baking parchment, so it won't stick to the bench. Spoon a layer of mushroom mixture onto the centre of each portion of the puff pastry. Place a slice of the pâté onto each pile of mushrooms, followed by the Roe deer loin and finally, one more spoonful of the mushroom mixture.

Lift the sides of pastry over the top of the filling before rolling each portion up into a parcel. Seal each parcel with the egg yolk wash and place on a tray lined with baking parchment. Finish by brushing with more egg yolk. Place in the fridge until ready to cook.

For The Red Wine, Port And Redcurrant Jelly Sauce

Caramelise the vegetables and herbs in a heavy bottomed pan with a little oil. *Deglaze* with the red wine then add the port. Reduce the liquor by half. Add the deer bones and cover with the stock. If there is not enough stock to cover the bones, top up with a little water. Bring the liquid to a boil and simmer for one to two hours. When the sauce is rich and has thickened slightly, pass the mixture through a sieve, into another pan and whisk in the redcurrant jelly. Bring the sauce back to a boil and transfer to a container to cool.

To Serve

Preheat an oven to 220°C. Put the deer parcels into the oven. Bake for 15 minutes, or until golden brown and crispy. Remove from the oven and leave to rest for five minutes before serving. Re-heat the sauce, slice the deer parcels into two halves and transfer to four warmed plates, with one side displaying the meat (the deer should be cooked rare to medium rare inside the pastry). Spoon the vegetables around the deer, then generously cover with the sauce.

BURNT NORTHUMBRIAN CREAMS

SERVES 4

🍷 *Elysium Black Muscat*
(California)

Ingredients

4 x 125ml dishes

600ml Northumbrian Pedigree whipping cream
1 vanilla pod (split and seeds scraped out)
50g caster sugar
5 large egg yolks
demerara sugar (to serve)

Method

Preheat oven to 100°C.

Whisk the egg yolks and sugar together until thick and doubled in volume.

Bring the cream and scraped vanilla pod to a boil and leave to infuse, off the heat, for at least one hour.

Return to the heat and heat until just boiling. Pour over the yolk and sugar mixture, whisking as you pour. Pass the mixture through a fine sieve, then place into four small 125ml dishes. Burst any bubbles with a blow torch, then place in an oven for 12 to 15 minutes until firm, but still wobbly. Remove from the oven and put to one side to cool. Refrigerate until needed.

To Serve

Sprinkle a thin layer of demerara sugar onto the top of the creams, tipping off any excess. Gently caramelise the sugar with a blowtorch. Leave to cool for one minute, until the topping hardens.

192
FOURTH FLOOR CAFE & BAR

Harvey Nichols, 107-111 Briggate, Leeds, LS1 6AZ

0113 204 8000
www.harveynichols.com

The Fourth Floor Café and Bar combines award-winning food and design for the perfect Leeds city centre dining experience. Situated on the top floor of Harvey Nichols, Leeds, the chic and striking Fourth Floor Café reflects the fashions in the floors below. Fusing contemporary with classic, the Café is opulent and dramatic, taking customers from day to night in a sweep of luxury. The stunning metallic shades, bronze-clad columns and deep teal leather seats all add to the room's allure, and a wall of windows reveals a striking rooftop vista.

The Fourth Floor's menus are a balance between the local and seasonal. The Café advocates local suppliers, ensuring its dishes exhibit the bounty and quality of produce available in Yorkshire. Seasonality is key and The Fourth Floor uses produce when it's at its peak. Changing each season, the Fourth Floor's menus showcase the delights of spring, fruits of summer, tastes of autumn and home cooked winter favourites.

Relish Restaurant Rewards
See page 003 for details.

With spectacular views over the city's rooftops, the Fourth Floor Café is an award-winning drinking and dining destination. With an interior that reflects the fashions in the floors below, the design of the Fourth Floor is opulent and dramatic, fusing contemporary with classic and taking customers from day to night in a sweep of luxury. Situated on the top floor of Harvey Nichols, Leeds, the Fourth Floor is the perfect city destination for breakfast, lunch, dinner and drinks.

HAND-DIVED ISLE OF MULL SCALLOPS IN A POTATO CRUST WITH TRUFFLE EMULSION, COASTAL HERBS & WHITE ASPARAGUS

SERVES 4

Harvey Nichols Sancerre 11
(France)

Ingredients

Scallops
6 scallops
potato airbag (de-hydrated potato - this has a
crumb like texture and is available online)
rapeseed oil (for deep frying)

Vegetables
8 white asparagus
coastal herbs and seaweed (selection of)
knob of butter

Dressing
1 large egg yolk
1 tsp sherry vinegar
$^1/_2$ tsp English mustard powder
sea salt (good pinch of)
white pepper (pinch of)
150ml olive oil
2 tsp truffle oil

Garnish
micro herbs
fresh truffle (optional)

Method

For The Dressing
Mix the egg yolk and vinegar, mustard and seasoning. Mix the oils together. Slowly add to the yolk mix whilst mixing until it thickens. If it's too thick loosen with warm water.

For The Scallops
Remove each scallop from its shell and clean cut the scallop in half around the waist. Blend the airbag potato to a fine crumb. Dip the scallop halves into the crumb. Deepfry in rapeseed oil for around 30 seconds until golden brown and puffed up.

For The Vegetables
Trim and prepare the asparagus, then finish in a pan with a knob of butter and a splash of water to create a cooking liquor. Clean the seaweed and herbs and panfry the same way.

To Serve
Work the plate with the truffle dressing, then build up with the vegetables and asparagus. Arrange three scallops per person on top of the vegetables. Garnish using the remaining seaweed and micro herbs. Finish with a shaving of fresh truffle, if available.

SLOW COOKED FILLET OF BEEF WITH OX TONGUE, GIROLLES, BABY ONIONS, SPRING PEAS, BLUE CHEESE CROQUETTE & SMOKED BONE MARROW SAUCE

SERVES 4

Harvey Nichols Plan de Dieu, Côtes du Rhône Villages 2009 (France)

Ingredients

Beef

4 x 5oz (approximately 140g) beef fillets
1 small cooked ox tongue (peeled and sliced)
knob of butter
4 sprigs rosemary

Vegetables

100g girolles
12 baby onions
100g spring peas

Blue Cheese Croquette

1 large jacket potato (baked and mashed)
Yorkshire blue cheese (wedge of)
Panko breadcrumbs
egg wash

Bone Marrow Sauce

100ml red wine sauce (can be bought ready made)
1 long piece smoked beef marrow

Garnish

pea shoots

Method

For The Blue Cheese Croquette

Mix the potato with the cheese, season and pipe into cylinders. Trim, shape, dip in egg wash, then roll in the breadcrumbs. Reserve until needed.

For The Vegetables

Clean the girolles. Peel the baby onions and cut in half. Pod the peas, *blanch* then refresh in iced water. Set aside.

For The Beef

Vacuum pack the beef with a knob of butter and the rosemary sprig. Cook in a water bath for approximately 20 to 22 minutes. The water needs to be set at 65°C. Alternatively, sear in a pan and roast in the oven for approximately eight minutes until cooked, or wrap in clingfilm and poach in warm water for 20 minutes to get the same effect.

Once cooked, remove from the pouch and sear in a hot pan. Season and leave to rest.

To Finish

In the same pan as the beef was cooked, sauté the tongue, peas, mushrooms and onions. Season and keep warm.

Whilst these are warming, slice the bone marrow into rounds and warm through in the red wine sauce. Deep fry the croquette until golden brown.

To Serve

Slice the beef in half and layer with the tongue in the centre of the plate. Work the onions, mushrooms and peas around the outside of the beef. Place the croquette next to the beef. Place a piece of marrow on top of the stack, then drizzle the sauce over and around. Garnish with the pea shoots. Enjoy!

202
GRAY'S RESTAURANT
AT THE WAREN HOUSE HOTEL

Bamburgh, Northumberland, NE70 7EE

01668 214 581
www.warenhousehotel.co.uk

Situated on the scenic coastal route of north Northumberland, The Waren House Hotel is privileged to be set amongst some of the most desirable and internationally renowned countryside in the UK. It is ideally located for our visitors to explore the delights of Northumberland and the Scottish Borders and is just two miles from the beautiful village of Bamburgh, seven miles from exploring the Cheviot Hills, or only 15 miles from the impressive Alnwick Castle and Gardens.

This enchanting Georgian House is described by our ever returning and loyal guests, as a 'perfect gem in a secret kingdom' - a statement in which we take great pride. This is seen in the efforts of our courteous and attentive staff.

Gastronomy is a subject we take very seriously. Our team of five dedicated chefs; Graham, David, Mark, Jamie and head chef Steven, work hard to deliver a dining experience we hope you won't forget. Our award-winning Gray's Restaurant is located in the heart of the hotel and is a favourite with guests and non-residents alike. We believe this is in part down to the use of only the finest locally sourced produce, obtained from suppliers within a 40 mile radius.

Our menu is complemented by an extensive wine list and we regularly receive high praise for our friendly and professional approach. All in all we believe The Waren House Hotel and Gray's Restaurant offers our guests a real 'home from home' experience.

Relish Restaurant Rewards
See page 003 for details.

PALET D'OR

SERVES 4

🍷 *Harvey Nichols LBV Port 08*
(Portugal)

Ingredients

Devil's Food Cake

100g plain flour
31g cocoa powder
2.5g bicarbonate of soda
0.5g baking powder
1g salt
56g eggs (approx 2 eggs - whisked)
126g granulated sugar
2g vanilla extract
86g mayonnaise

Pâte á Glacer

333ml double cream
233g dark chocolate (at least 70% chocolate mass)
50g eggs
100g egg yolks
83g granulated sugar

Chocolate Mirror Glaze

7.2g gelatine
150ml double cream
225g granulated sugar
180ml water
75g cocoa powder

4 metal ring moulds (7.5cm x 3.5cm)

Method

For The Cake

Preheat oven to 162°C. Sieve the flour, cocoa, bicarbonate of soda, baking powder and salt. Whisk the eggs, sugar and vanilla for five minutes until pale. Add the mayonnaise. Fold in the dry ingredients. Add a little water if required. Bake, using a flat tray lined with silicone paper, for ten minutes. The cake mix needs to be around 10mm thick before baking.

For The Pâte á Glacer

Whip the cream to form soft peaks then chill and reserve. Whisk the eggs, egg yolk and sugar in a pan until it reaches 83°C. Whisk until cool.

Melt the chocolate to 48°C. Fold one third of the cream in with the chocolate and then fold into the egg mix. Fold in the rest of the cream.

To Build The Cakes (Prepare the day before)

Take a metal mousse ring and cut out the cakes. You will need three discs cut out from the devils food cake to build each individual cake - they need to be smaller than the ring mould used to build the cakes so as not to come into contact with the edges of the mould. Trim the cakes so that they are nice and flat. You will need four round metal rings to build the cakes. Put the first disc into the bottom, then pipe the pâte á glacer onto and around the cake, then place another round on top and repeat. Top with the third cake layer and cover the remaining space with the mixture, smooth off and freeze overnight. When piping the pâte á glacer, make sure that there aren't any gaps on the outside edge as this will affect the final appearance of the Palet d'Or.

For The Chocolate Mirror Glaze

Bring the cream, sugar and water to a boil then whisk in the cocoa. Boil gently for around 15 minutes until it is reduced by half. Soften the gelatine in cold water and then dissolve in the reduced mixture.

To Serve

Remove the cakes from the moulds and place on a cooling rack. Pour over the mirror glaze, making sure that you coat the cakes evenly. Let the mixture set, then leave to defrost until needed. Use a pallet knife to carefully transfer the cake to each plate. The cake will keep fresh in the fridge for a couple of days in an airtight container. Serve chilled.

Chef's Tip

The Devil's Food cake needs freezing for several hours before serving. We serve it with a blood orange sorbet and gold leaf in the restaurant, but try it with different things at home. A good vanilla ice cream works well.

202
GRAY'S
RESTAURANT
AT THE WAREN HOUSE HOTEL

Bamburgh, Northumberland, NE70 7EE

01668 214 581
www.warenhousehotel.co.uk

ituated on the scenic coastal route of north Northumberland, The Waren House Hotel is privileged to be set amongst some of the most desirable and internationally renowned countryside in the UK. It is ideally located for our visitors to explore the delights of Northumberland and the Scottish Borders and is just two miles from the beautiful village of Bamburgh, seven miles from exploring the Cheviot Hills, or only 15 miles from the impressive Alnwick Castle and Gardens.

This enchanting Georgian House is described by our ever returning and loyal guests, as a 'perfect gem in a secret kingdom' - a statement in which we take great pride. This is seen in the efforts of our courteous and attentive staff.

Gastronomy is a subject we take very seriously. Our team of five dedicated chefs; Graham, David, Mark, Jamie and head chef Steven, work hard to deliver a dining experience we hope you won't forget. Our award-winning Gray's Restaurant is located in the heart of the hotel and is a favourite with guests and non-residents alike. We believe this is in part down to the use of only the finest locally sourced produce, obtained from suppliers within a 40 mile radius.

Our menu is complemented by an extensive wine list and we regularly receive high praise for our friendly and professional approach. All in all we believe The Waren House Hotel and Gray's Restaurant offers our guests a real 'home from home' experience.

Relish Restaurant Rewards
See page 003 for details.

Steven and his team of four chefs
are all Northumbrian born and
bred and are passionate about
using the best locally sourced
ingredients in Northumberland.
This is reflected in their culinary
creations on a daily basis.

THYME BREADED RABBIT, CITRUS PICKLED CARROT, GIROLLES, RED CHARD, RABBIT SAUCE

SERVES 4

🍷 *Willowglen Chardonnay (Australia)*

Ingredients

Thyme Breaded Rabbit

2 rabbit saddles (loins removed giving 4 loins)
2 eggs (mixed and strained)
2 slices dried bread
plain flour
2 sprigs fresh thyme

Sauce

stock (made using the rabbit saddle bones)
1 shallot (chopped)
50ml white wine
50ml Madeira wine
1 sprig thyme
girolles
knob of butter

Vinaigrette

50ml orange juice
50ml lemon juice
1 tsp Dijon mustard
1 tsp caster sugar
salt (to taste)
100ml rapeseed oil

Garnish

1 carrot
red chard leaves

Method

For The Thyme Breaded Rabbit

Put the dried bread in a blender with the thyme leaves and blend.

Remove the sinew from the rabbit loins and pass through the flour, egg and then the breadcrumbs. Shallow fry until just cooked.

> **Chef's Tip**
> Fry the rabbit last minute to avoid it being dry.

For The Sauce

Brush a pan with oil and fry the shallot without colouring. Add girolles and cook. Add white wine and Madeira wine then reduce by half. Add the sprig of thyme and rabbit stock and reduce until sticky. Add a knob of butter to finish.

For The Vinaigrette

Blend all the vinaigrette ingredients together until it *emulsifies*.

For The Garnish

Peel then slice the carrot thinly on a mandolin and *blanch* in boiling water. Remove and add to cold water before putting into the vinaigrette to soak for at least four hours.

To Serve

Slice a rabbit loin into pieces and arrange on the plate. Add some red chard leaves with the vinaigrette, carrot ribbons, girolles and sauce. Enjoy!

ROAST DUCK BREAST, DUCK LEG CRUMBLE, SOY HONEY PUMPKIN SEED VEGETABLES, PLUM, BUTTERNUT & WILTED SPINACH

SERVES 4

Pinot Noir, Domaine de Coussergues d'Oc
(France)

Ingredients

Duck

1 duck
1 carrot (chopped)
1 onion (chopped)
1 star anise
1 bay leaf
1 stick of celery (chopped)

Vegetable Julienne with Pumpkin Seeds

1 red pepper (*julienne*)
1/2 onion (sliced finely)
1 carrot (*julienne*)
1 head spring greens (chopped finely)
1 leek (cut thinly)
4 tbsp pumpkin seeds
30g butter

Soy Honey Dressing

50ml soy sauce
100ml runny honey

Roast Butternut

butternut squash
rapeseed oil

Spinach

1 bag spinach
25g butter

Roast Plums

2 tart plums (halved)
4 tsp runny honey

Method

For The Duck (Cook overnight)

Remove the duck legs and score the skin of the breasts. Put the legs in a pan with the vegetables, spices and herbs then cover with water and place a lid on top. Transfer to the oven and cook at 120°C overnight.

For The Duck Reduction

When the duck is cooked, strain the stock. Allow to settle then skim off the fat.

Reduce the stock until sticky, reserving half for the sauce. Remove the duck meat from the legs and heat with the remaining stock. Keep warm.

For The Roast Butternut

Peel the butternut and chop into 1cm dice. Roast in a pan with some rapeseed oil and season.

For The Spinach

Wilt the spinach leaves in butter.

For The Roast Plums

Roast the plums in the runny honey for five minutes at 180°C.

For Soy Honey Dressing

Mix the soy sauce with the honey.

To Serve

Heat a sauté pan. Add duck breasts, skin side down, for two to three minutes, then turn over. Cook until pink. Rest.

Sauté the vegetables in butter with pumpkin seeds and 40ml of the soy and honey dressing.

Arrange the *julienne* of vegetables in a small mould with the sliced duck breast on top. Place the duck leg *confit* meat in a smaller mould. Toast some ground pumpkin seeds and place on top of leg mix. Garnish with the butternut, plums, spinach and reserved duck reduction.

> **Chef's Tip**
> Leave breast to rest for a couple of minutes before slicing.

DARK CHOCOLATE FONDANT, WHITE CHOCOLATE SORBET, CHOCOLATE STREUSEL, CREME FRAICHE

SERVES 4

🍷 *Muscat Beaumes -de-Venise N.V.*
(France)

Ingredients

Chocolate Fondant

170g dark chocolate
110g unsalted butter
125g eggs
75g egg yolks
60g plain flour
75g caster sugar

White Chocolate Sorbet

100g white chocolate
140ml water
15g liquid glucose

Streusel

20g chocolate (chopped)
40g plain flour
20g cocoa powder
25g butter
25g brown sugar

To Serve

crème fraîche
dark chocolate (melted to make chocolate case)

Method

For The Chocolate Fondant

Melt the chocolate and butter in a bowl, over a pan of boiling water. Whisk the eggs, egg yolks and sugar in a mixing bowl until stiff peaks are formed. Add the flour, then fold in the chocolate and butter - mix by hand. Place into non-stick individual pudding moulds, filling the moulds to about 0.5cm from the top. Bake at 180°C for eight minutes.

> **Chef's Tip**
>
> Serve the fondant as quickly as possible as the centre will keep on cooking and needs to be runny when served.

For The White Chocolate Sorbet

Melt the white chocolate, water and liquid glucose in a pan. Remove from the heat and cool. Churn in an ice cream machine.

For The Streusel

Rub all ingredients together (except for the chocolate) and bake on a non-stick mat in an oven at 160°C for 20 minutes. Now add the chopped chocolate pieces and return to the oven for a further five minutes. Remove from oven and, when cooled, lightly blend.

To Serve

Remove the fondant from the mould - do be careful as it is hot, especially the soft centre. Serve with a scoop of sorbet on a bed of streusel and add a dollop of crème fraîche served in a chocolate case - formed by brushing some melted chocolate around a silicone mould and allowed to set.

212
HEADLAM HALL

Headlam, Near Gainford, Darlington, County Durham, DL2 3HA

01325 730 238
www.headlamhall.co.uk

Headlam Hall is a charming Jacobean country manor house in lower Teesdale, standing in delightful walled gardens and surrounded by its own rolling farmland. This family owned and run hotel has built its reputation around great food served in a fantastic setting. The hall itself dates back to the mid-17th Century and there is plenty to remind you of its rich history. On walking through the large old oak door you will discover stone flagged floors, large open fireplaces and fitting antiques adorning the welcoming rooms.

The restaurant offers diners a choice of the warm and intimate Panelled Room or the more contemporary Orangery which is surrounded by a secluded patio area, giving the option of al fresco dining. There is also good scope for private dining and the beautiful Georgian styled drawing room opens onto a stepped terrace overlooking the immaculate main lawns. You can enjoy a pre-dinner drink in the cosy cocktail bar and after dinner coffee and liqueurs in the impressive main hall lounge that features stone pillars and the original carved oak fireplace.

The four acres of walled gardens are a real feature of this country house with colourful herbaceous borders, an ornamental canal and a productive kitchen garden amidst the ancient beech hedges. The hotel also offers 39 bedrooms, an award-winning spa and a challenging nine-hole golf course to keep you amused.

Relish Restaurant Rewards
See page 003 for details.

The kitchen team, led by David Hunter, has the ability to produce great food for both intimate fine dining and lavish dinner parties. The chefs have long standing relationships with excellent local suppliers and are always looking at new ideas on how to showcase the great local ingredients. They also enjoy using seasonal fruit, vegetables and herbs grown in the hall gardens and lamb reared on the Robinson's family farm. Food awards include two AA rosettes and Taste Durham Highest Quality Assured and Local Champion.

PANFRIED FILLET OF HALIBUT WITH SMOKED AUBERGINE, CONFIT CHICKEN WING, BAKED HERITAGE CARROTS, BROWN SHRIMPS & CHICKEN JUS

SERVES 4

Muscadet Sur Lie, Clos de Chapelle, 2010
(France)

Ingredients

4 x 120g pieces halibut (skinned)
rapeseed oil (for frying)

Aubergine

1 large aubergine
salt and pepper

Chicken Wings

4 chicken wings (middle part only)
duck fat (enough to cover)
clear honey (for brushing)

2 Heritage carrots
100g brown shrimps
100ml chicken jus
knob of butter

Garnish

nasturtium leaves
fresh herbs

Method

For The Aubergine

Burn the aubergine on a naked gas flame until black all over and cooked. Scrape the inside of the aubergine out into a food processor. Season with salt and pepper. Blitz until smooth.

For The Chicken Wings

Cover the wings with duck fat and cook in the oven at 100°C for one hour. Push out the bones while still hot. Season and brush with honey.

For The Carrots

Peel, season and roast the carrots. When cool enough to handle, cut into desired shapes.

To Serve

Season and panfry the halibut in rapeseed oil for three minutes, then add a knob of butter. Turn, then add carrots and brown shrimps to the pan and leave to rest. Place the chicken wings under a hot grill until brown and hot. Heat the aubergine in a small saucepan.

Plate as desired and finish with the chicken jus, nasturtium leaves and herbs.

PANFRIED LOIN OF VENISON WITH TEXTURES OF SHALLOT, FONDANT POTATO, WILTED WILD GARLIC & A VENISON JUS

SERVES 4

🍷 *Syrah Matakana Estate, 2009*
(New Zealand)

Ingredients

Fondant Potatoes

150g butter
4 potatoes (peeled and cut into barrel shapes
using a cookie cutter)
75ml chicken or vegetable stock
2 cloves garlic (peeled and lightly crushed with
the edge of a knife)
2 - 3 sprigs fresh thyme

Venison

4 x 175g venison loin (fully trimmed)
1 tbsp olive oil
1 sprig thyme
1 clove garlic (crushed)

Shallot Purée

350g shallots (finely chopped)
300ml chicken stock
knob of butter
1 tbsp olive oil

Wild Garlic

12 large leaves wild garlic
10g unsalted butter
4 tbsp water

sea salt flakes
black pepper (freshly ground)

To Serve

roasted shallots
venison jus
wild garlic flowers

Method

For The Potatoes

Heat the butter over a medium heat in a saucepan. When the butter is foaming, add the potatoes and fry until deep golden brown on one side, about five to six minutes. Turn over the potatoes and cook for a further five to six minutes, or until golden brown on both sides. Carefully pour in the stock and then add the garlic cloves and thyme sprigs. Season to taste with salt and black pepper. Cover the pan with a lid and reduce the heat until the stock is simmering. Simmer the potatoes until tender, then remove the potatoes from the pan using a slotted spoon and keep warm.

For The Venison

Preheat the oven to 180°C. Heat a large, ovenproof frying pan and fry the venison until golden brown all over. Place in the oven with the oil and herbs and cook for four to six minutes, or until cooked to your liking. Remove from the oven, cover with a warm plate and leave to rest for five minutes.

For The Shallot Purée

Heat the butter and olive oil together in a frying pan until foaming and gently fry the shallots for nine to ten minutes, or until very tender. Pour in the stock and bring to a boil. Cook for ten minutes or until the shallots begin to break down. Strain the shallots, reserving a few tablespoons of the cooking liquid and place into a food processor. Blend with the reserved cooking liquid until smooth. Scrape into a bowl and season to taste with salt and freshly ground black pepper. Set aside.

For The Wilted Wild Garlic

Wash the wild garlic leaves in cold water. Cut the leaves with a sharp knife into strips. Add the water and the butter to a pan and bring to a boil with a pinch of salt. When the water is boiling, add the wild garlic and cook until the water has evaporated and the leaves have a wonderful shine.

To Serve

Serve with roasted shallots, wild garlic flowers and venison jus.

LEMON

SERVES 6

🍷 *Chateau le Fleur d'Or, Sauternes
(France)*

Ingredients

Lemons

6 lemons
basic sugar syrup (enough to cover)

Lemon Curd

4 large eggs
350g caster sugar
225g butter (cut into small dice)
1 dtsp cornflour
4 lemons (juice of)

Panna Cotta

3 lemons
600ml double cream
150ml milk
200g caster sugar
2 lemons (zest and juice of)
1 lime (zest of)
3 leaves gelatine (softened in cold water)

To Serve

lemon sorbet
homemade shortbread

Method

For The Lemons (Prepare three days before)

Bring six whole lemons to a simmer in the syrup. Turn down the heat and cook until soft. Leave in the syrup for three days to soak up some sweetness.

For The Lemon Curd

Begin by lightly whisking the eggs in a medium-sized saucepan. Add the rest of the ingredients and place the saucepan over a medium heat. Whisk continuously using a balloon whisk until the mixture thickens – about seven to eight minutes. Next, lower the heat to its minimum setting and let the curd gently simmer for a further minute, continuing to whisk. After that, remove it from the heat. Pour the lemon curd into hot, sterilised jars, filling them as full as possible. Cover straightaway with waxed discs.
Seal while it is still hot and label when it is cold. It will keep for several weeks, but it must be stored in a cool place.

For The Panna Cotta

Put the cream, milk and sugar into a large pan and bring slowly to a boil. When the cream is boiling, add the lemon juice and the lemon and lime zest and whisk well. Simmer for a few minutes until reduced slightly then turn off the heat.

Scoop the softened gelatine out of the water and squeeze out any excess water. Stir into the hot cream. Leave until just warm, then strain the cream into a jug.

To Serve (Prepare at least five hours before)

Make a small hole in the bottom of each lemon and scoop out the insides. Fill with the lemon curd and lemon panna cotta and place in the fridge for at least five hours until completely set - overnight is ideal. Serve with lemon sorbet and homemade shortbread.

222
THE JOLLY FISHERMAN

Haven Hill, Craster, Northumberland, NE66 3TR

01665 576 461
www.thejollyfishermancraster.co.uk

The Jolly Fisherman, Craster, combines stunning sea views with delicious home cooking and beautifully kept ales. A tastefully refurbished pub with tradition and character at its heart.

Great care has been taken to retain the charm of this historic pub with stone flagged floors, low beamed ceilings and comfortable seating. Large sliding windows, overlooking the harbour, give the feeling of being outside. Enjoy the terrace and beer garden during the summer months, with unrivalled views of the coastline and during the winter, relax by the roaring, open fires.

Fresh crab and lobster is delivered daily from the last remaining fishing boat out of Craster. Local game and meats are sourced from surrounding Northumberland Estates.

The Jolly Fisherman was established by Charles Archbold in 1847. Over the past 165 years, the building has grown in both size and reputation and is popular with locals, coastal ramblers and day-trippers alike.

Following a full refurbishment in 2012, new publican David Whitehead, and his team, are proud to continue and enhance the rich culinary heritage of one of Northumberland's most iconic destinations.

Relish Restaurant Rewards
See page 003 for details.

Great care has been taken to retain the charm of this historic pub with stone flagged floors, low beamed ceilings and comfortable seating.

JOLLY FISHERMAN'S FISH BOARD

SERVES 4

🍷 *2012 Domaine Félines Jourdan, Picpoul de Pinet (France)*

Ingredients

Fish

2 fillets smoked trout
2 fillets smoked mackerel
4 slices smoked salmon

Potted Brown Shrimp

125g brown shrimp
30g butter (*clarified*)
dill (sprinkling of)

Kipper Mousse

110g kipper fillet
2 tbsp cream cheese
1 tbsp double cream

Garnish

4 slices brown sourdough bread (cut in half)
60g unsalted butter (or 4 x 15g)
1 tsp sea salt
salad leaves
micro fennel
1 lime

8 ramekins (5cm)

Method

For The Fish

Cut the smoked trout and mackerel in half. Lightly roll out the smoked salmon and set aside in fridge.

For The Potted Brown Shrimp

Mix the shrimp with the lime juice and dill. Divide into four 5cm ramekins.

For The Kipper Mousse

Steam the kipper for a few minutes until cooked. Cool, then remove the skin and break up into pieces. Fold in the cream and cream cheese, then add into the four ramekins. Set in the fridge for ten minutes.

For The Clarified Butter

Melt the butter and skim off any impurities, leaving a clear butter. Pour the *clarified* butter on top of the shrimp mix and place the four pots to set in the fridge for ten minutes.

To Serve

Arrange the salad leaves and micro fennel in the centre of a slate. Place the fish and potted shrimp around the leaves and serve with a wedge of lime, brown sourdough bread, butter and sea salt.

STONE BASS WITH CAPER MASH, SUN BLUSHED TOMATO SALSA, BRAISED LEEKS

SERVES 4

Montes Sauvignon Blanc, 2012
(Chile)

Ingredients

Stone Bass Fillet
200g Stone Bass fillet (cut into 4 x 50g pieces)
125g butter

Caper Mash
300g King Edward potatoes
10g capers
50g unsalted butter

Salsa
80g dried sun-blushed tomatoes
120g cherry tomatoes
1 shallot (finely diced)
6 basil leaves (torn)
100ml olive oil

Garnish
micro herbs
1 large leek (cut into 4 and cooked in vegetable stock for five minutes)

Maldon sea salt and ground black pepper
(to season)

Method

For The Stone Bass
Coat each of the four pieces of Stone Bass in butter. Cook in the oven for ten minutes at 180°C.

For The Caper Mash
Peel and slice the potatoes evenly. Cook in boiling water until soft. Strain, add butter then mash thoroughly. Mix in the capers and season.

For The Salsa
Chop the tomatoes and mix with the finely diced shallot and olive oil. Leave to marinate for at least two hours. Add the torn basil leaves just before serving.

To Serve
Arrange the braised leeks and top with the mash, using a ring to shape. Arrange the warmed Stone Bass on top and finish with the salsa. Garnish with micro herbs and a drizzle of oil from the tomato salsa.

LEMON POSSET & SHORTBREAD

SERVES 4

🍷 *Amaretto*
(Italy)

Ingredients

Lemon Posset
600ml double cream
170g caster sugar
2 lemons (zest and juice)

Shortbread
130g plain flour
50g caster sugar
100g butter
20g cornflour

Garnish
lime wedges
raspberries

Method

For The Lemon Posset
Heat the cream and sugar gently for four minutes. Set aside to cool. Add lemon zest and juice into the cooled mixture. Whisk thoroughly until a creamy consistency is reached.

Divide into four martini glasses and leave to set in the fridge for at least three hours.

For The Shortbread
Preheat the oven to 180°C.

Sift the icing sugar, flour and cornflour together into a bowl.

Transfer the flour mixture to a food processor. Add the butter and pulse until there are no visible lumps of butter.

Grease a tray. Roll out the dough to 4mm thick and cut into rounds.

Cook in oven for ten minutes.

To Serve
Assemble as in picture.

LOTUS LOUNGE

Fairfax Court, 32-34 High Street, Yarm, TS15 9AE

01642 355 558
www.lotus-lounge.co.uk

Situated down a busy shopping arcade in the famous High Street, Lotus Lounge is a relatively new addition to Yarm's restaurant scene, offering pan-Asian cuisine.

On the ground floor, a café bar serves food daily from 9am, while the restaurant above is open five nights a week, offering a fine dining experience.

Lotus Lounge provides diners with the chance to sample authentic dishes from across Asia in a relaxed setting of deep oak furniture, orchids and Buddha statues.

Our vibrant, relaxed dining experience has proved to be a great draw for diners in the region, with the restaurant being booked up weeks in advance.

The kitchen team is led by executive chef Martin Moore, who draws on his experience heading up another of the region's pan-Asian successes - The Ozone Restaurant at Seaham Hall.

Our well travelled chefs have a wealth of experience in Eastern and Asian food, which is all about the freshness of ingredients and pace of cooking.

Our menu is based on Asian fusion which brings together a host of ingredients, flavours and preparation methods.

We carefully source our ingredients, to create a finished look and taste which is totally fresh and new.

Lotus Lounge is well worth a visit next time you are in Yarm!

Relish Restaurant Rewards
See page 003 for details.

The second in the expanding restaurant group, Lotus Lounge Durham, is situated on bustling Saddler Street, on the way up to the Cathedral.

The new kitchen team is headed by Lee Hardy, who joined the Lotus Lounge team a year ago.

"Having travelled around China, and previously worked in Hong Kong, Shanghai, Beijing and Shenzen, I have developed a great passion for Asian cooking," says Lee. "I am looking forward to creating a well-established name for the company and I want people to hear 'Lotus Lounge' and automatically think of a quality dining experience."

Our varied menu offers light Asian tapas - from Dim Sums to Pad Thai, tied in with classic main dishes drawn from Japanese, Thai, Chinese, and Vietnamese cuisines.

Lotus Lounge Restaurants have become synonymous with top quality pan-Asian food, served in stylish, informal surroundings. We focus on using the best locally sourced produce to create an enticing blend of flavours from China, Japan and Thailand; and on introducing Asian street food flavours to our fresh, innovative and well-presented dishes of refined eastern cuisine.

PAD THAI

SERVES 2

Finca Los Tranzones Verdejo 2011
(Spain)

Ingredients

Chicken

1 x 200g skinless chicken breast (sliced)
100ml chicken stock
garlic
fresh chilli (optional)

250g Thai rice noodles 10mm (or enough for 2)
(available at Asian and Chinese stores)

Marinade for Chicken

1 tsp cornstarch
3 tbsp sweet soy sauce
4 cloves garlic (crushed)
1-2 fresh red chillies (finely chopped, optional)

Pad Thai Sauce

50 ml Pad Thai sauce (250ml bottle)
(Pantai brand, sold in most Asian, Chinese or
Indian food stores)
2 tsp fish sauce (plus more to taste)
1-3 tsp chilli sauce (or more dried crushed chilli)

Vegetables

100g fresh bean sprouts
1 small red onion (sliced)
$1/4$ red pepper (sliced)
1 medium egg

vegetable or sesame oil (for stir-frying)

Garnish

20g fresh coriander
2 spring onions (sliced)
40g peanuts (crushed or roughly chopped)
lime wedges
Nam Prik Pao chilli sauce (optional)

Method

Chef's Tip

A fast, easy version of Pad Thai. The key to perfect Pad Thai is the cooking (or 'not' cooking) of the noodles. Included is a simple, but authentic Pad Thai sauce which is tangy and a little spicy. When all put together, you'll find there isn't a noodle dish better than world-famous Pad Thai!

Prep time: approx 15 minutes, cook time: approx 12 minutes, total time: approx 30 minutes.

For The Noodles

Bring a large pot of water to a boil and dunk in your rice noodles. Turn down the heat to low and keep an eye on them - you will be frying the noodles later, so you don't want to over-soften them now. Noodles are ready to be drained when they are soft enough to be eaten, but still firm and a little 'crunchy'. Drain and rinse with cold water to prevent sticking. Set aside.

For The Chicken

Place the chicken slices in a small bowl. Stir together the marinade and pour over the chicken. Stir well and set aside.

Warm up a wok or large frying pan over medium-high heat. Add one to two tablespoons of oil plus garlic and finely chopped chilli (optional). Stir-fry until fragrant (30 seconds). Add the marinated chicken. When the wok or pan becomes dry, add a little chicken stock (one to two tablespoons at a time), to keep the chicken frying nicely (five to seven minutes) until cooked.

For The Pad Thai Sauce

Combine all the ingredients together. Set aside.

For The Vegetables

Add the red onion and peppers to the wok. Stir-fry for 30 seconds until they soften, then add the *blanched* rice noodles. Stir-fry for another minute, then pour the Pad Thai sauce over. With tongs, use a gentle 'lift and turn' method to fry the noodles (like tossing a salad). Stir-fry in this way for one to two minutes. If you find your wok or frying pan is too dry, push the noodles aside and add a little more Pad Thai sauce to the pan.

Add the bean sprouts and egg and continue frying for one more minute, or until the noodles and egg are cooked. Noodles are done to perfection when they are no longer 'hard' or crunchy, but chewy-sticky wonderful! Taste test for seasoning, adding more fish sauce until a desired flavour is reached (I usually add one more tablespoon of fish sauce). Toss well to incorporate.

To Serve

Lift noodles onto two warmed serving plates or Asian-style bowls. Top with generous amounts of fresh coriander, spring onion and crushed or chopped nuts. Drizzle Pad Thai sauce over the dish, add fresh lime wedges to squeeze, and, if desired, serve with Nam Prik Pao chilli sauce on the side. Enjoy!

BLACKENED MISO COD, UDON NOODLE & VEGETABLE BROTH

SERVES 2

Luis Felipe Edward Chardonnay 2012
(Chile)

Ingredients

Miso Stock

75g miso paste (Marukome Boy, koshi)
300ml water or vegetable stock
3 tbsp sweet soy sauce (Healthy Boy)
2 star anise
2 sticks lemongrass (sliced)
1 thumb ginger (sliced or diced)
20g coriander stalks (chopped)

Cod

1 tbsp butter
1 tbsp toasted sesame oil (Silk Road)
2 x 200g square cut local cod fillets
2 tbsp sweet soy sauce (Healthy Boy)
1 tbsp sweet chilli sauce (Healthy Boy)

Noodle And Vegetable Broth

200g (1 pack) udon noodles (fuku Japanese)
1 red chilli pepper (seeded and thinly sliced)
4 spring onions (thinly sliced)
1 shitake mushroom (sliced)
6 spears new season asparagus (peeled, trimmed
and *blanched*)
50g bean sprouts

Garnish

coriander leaves

Method

> **Chef's Tip**
> The stock is an important element to this dish. Strong flavours and tastes are released by slow simmering to make great broth and complete the dish.
> Prep time: 15 minutes, cook time: 20 minutes

For The Miso Stock

Into a wok or large saucepan, add the miso paste, water or stock, three tablespoons of soy sauce and the other ingredients. Bring to a boil, and then reduce the heat to simmer for ten minutes, allowing the flavours to infuse.

While the miso stock is infusing, prepare the cod.

For The Cod

Melt the butter and sesame oil in a pan. Add the cod fillets, searing them over a medium-high heat. Turn fillets over. Baste the cod with sweet soy sauce and sweet chilli sauce, to glaze. Reduce heat to medium and cook for an additional five to six minutes. Continue to baste the cod, to enrich flavours and colour, until opaque throughout.

For The Noodle And Vegetable Broth

Add the noodles to the miso stock and cook for five minutes. Add the chilli, spring onions, mushrooms, bean sprouts and asparagus and cook for an additional two minutes. Ladle the noodle mixture into two wide bowls, (remove the star anise) and top with a cod fillet. Serve with the cooking juices over the cod, dress with fresh coriander.

(see glossary)

THAI SWEET RICE PUDDING, MANGO CHUTNEY

SERVES 4

🍷 *'Tom Yam Siam' is a Patron Cocktail*

Ingredients

Rice Pudding

250g pudding rice
$1/4$ tsp salt
1 x 400ml can good quality (thick) coconut milk
1 tbsp caster sugar
2 stick lemongrass (bashed)
2 star anise
4 mint leaves or lime leaves (roughly torn)
500ml water

Mango Chutney

1 ripe mango (cut into bite-size pieces, or tinned is fine)
4-5 tbsp caster or brown sugar
4 mint leaves or lime leaves (roughly torn)
$1/2$ tsp dry ginger
25 ml honey

Garnish

shaved coconut

Method

This mango sticky rice dessert (Khao Niaow Ma Muang) is a classic Thai dessert and so very scrumptious. Be sure to get the right rice for this dessert - regular (savoury) rice will not work; you need sweet rice. The sticky rice can either be steamed, as they do in Thailand (a colander can be used for this), or you can make it in a pot on your stove. Place some fresh mango chutney over the coconut infused sticky rice. Pure heaven!

If you like mangos and sticky rice, you're going to love this very simple but exotic Thai dessert.

> **Chef's Tip**
>
> Slow, gentle cooking and stirring will release the Asian flavours and will not break down the rice.
>
> Prep time: 10 minutes, cook time: 25 minutes, total time: 35 minutes

For The Rice Pudding

Soak the rice in 300ml water for 20 to 30 minutes. Drain. Into a heavy bottomed pan, add 400ml of coconut milk and 200ml water, quarter of a teaspoon of salt and one tablespoon of caster sugar. Stir this into the rice. Add the lemongrass, star anise and mint or lime leaves.

Bring to a gentle boil, and then partially cover with a lid (leaving some room for steam to escape). Reduce heat to medium-low.

Simmer for 15 to 20 minutes, or until the coconut milk and water has been absorbed by the rice. Add more water if required. Turn off the heat, but leave the pot on the burner with the lid on tight. Leave to sit for five to ten minutes.

For The Mango Chutney

Put the diced mangos and three tablespoons of sugar in a small pan on a low heat and stir until the sugar has dissolved. Add the dry ginger, honey and the rest of the mint leaves. Gently cook for five minutes until softened. If it gets dry, add some water to loosen the chutney.

Taste-test the chutney for sweetness, adding more sugar if desired. (Note that it will taste less sweet when added to the rice).

To Serve

Place mounds of sticky rice in each warm serving bowl. Top with mango chutney, then pour any liquid sauce around and over the rice.

Sprinkle with a few coconut shavings and enjoy!

THE MAGPIE CAFE

14 Pier Road, Whitby, North Yorkshire, YO21 3PU

01947 602 058
www.magpiecafe.co.uk

The harbour side in the historic port of Whitby has been the home of The Magpie Café for over 70 years.

Built in 1750 as the home of a local merchant, the property has served many functions, including being the pilotage where the pilots would wait to guide ships into the harbour and the offices of the Harrowing shipping company, before finally becoming The Magpie in 1939.

As a family run restaurant, we have always endeavoured to create an informal, relaxed setting and to offer great food at an affordable price.

Whilst we are probably best known for our fish and chips, diners are often surprised to see the variety of dishes on offer.

Given our proximity to the North Sea and the local fish market, it will come as no surprise that we specialise in fresh, locally caught (whenever possible) fish and seafood, but carnivores and vegetarians are well catered for too - both are on the main menu and the frequently changing specials board.

It is not unusual for us to have a dozen varieties of fresh fish on offer, from cod and haddock through to halibut and John Dory, plus Whitby crab and lobster and of course the famous Whitby kipper.

We have an excellent wine list to complement the food and around 15 homemade desserts.

Although the restaurant caters for up to 120 diners, the seating is spread across a number of rooms so it never feels too big!

Relish Restaurant Rewards
See page 003 for details.

Ian Robson, head chef Paul Gildroy and their kitchen team have received much critical acclaim over the years from food guides and journalists, most notably The Good Food Guide (33 years continuous entry) and Hardens UK Restaurant Guide.

Friendly and efficient front of house service is overseen by Alison Slater and Duncan Robson.

"As a family run restaurant we have always endeavoured to create an informal, relaxed setting and to offer great food at an affordable price".

MEDALLIONS OF MONKFISH ON SWEET POTATO WITH GOAT'S CHEESE, SCALLIONS & A CIDER GLAZE

SERVES 4

🍷 *Jansz Premium Cuvee. Pipers Brook (Northern Tasmania)*

Ingredients

Monkfish

400g monkfish (trimmed and off the bone - cut into 12 medallions)
8 spring onions (scallions)
oil (for panfrying)

Potato Purée

400g sweet potatoes
1 clove garlic
knob of butter
salt and pepper

Cider Syrup

200ml dry cider
2 tbsp sugar

200g goat's cheese (sliced very thinly, or crumbled)

Method

For The Sweet Potato Purée

Peel and roughly chop the sweet potatoes and crush the garlic, bring to a boil in a pan of salted water and cook until tender. Drain and blitz in a food processor with the knob of butter until very smooth. Pass through a sieve and season with salt and pepper.

For The Cider Syrup

In a pan, heat the cider with the sugar, bring to a boil and reduce to thin syrup. Set aside.

For The Monkfish And Spring Onion

Heat a large frying or sauté pan, drizzle in a little oil. Season the monkfish with salt and pepper then lay into the pan, clockwise. Over a high heat cook the monkfish for one minute, then turn each piece over again, working clockwise round the pan and cook for a further minute. Remove the monkfish from the pan and keep warm. Cut the spring onions in half and split lengthways. Add to the pan and lightly sauté for 30 seconds or so. Add the cider syrup.

> **Chef's Tip**
> Make sure to cut the medallions to an even thickness to ensure consistent and even cooking of each piece.

To Serve

Place a tablespoon of sweet potato purée onto each plate and drag the spoon across the top. Place three monkfish medallions per plate on the potato purée, then share the spring onions (scallions) between the plates. Arrange the goat's cheese and finish by drizzling over the cider syrup.

SEAFOOD MEDLEY

SERVES 4

🍷 *Sauvignon Blanc – Wild Rock Infamous Goose*
Marlborough (New Zealand)

Ingredients

Fish

4 x 100g fillets wild salmon (if wild is not available we recommend Loch Duart farmed salmon)
4 x 100g turbot fillet
8 king scallops
8 king prawns

Potato

1kg good mashing potatoes
4 cloves garlic
handful fresh parsley (chopped)
50ml double cream
75ml milk
50g butter

Samphire

140g fresh samphire grass
4 shallots (finely sliced)
200ml double cream
50g butter

Garnish

fresh micro herbs (these are available at most good greengrocers)

oil (for panfrying)
salt and pepper

Method

For The Potato

Peel and roughly chop the potatoes, place into a pan of salted water, cover with a lid and bring to a boil. When the potatoes are nearly cooked, crush the garlic and add to the potatoes. Continue to cook until tender, strain off any excess water. Mash the potatoes with 50g of butter and 75ml of milk until smooth. Add 50ml of double cream, finish with the chopped parsley and season with salt and pepper.

For The Fish

Heat a large ovenproof pan, add a little oil and gently lay the salmon followed by the turbot, both flesh side down. Cook for approximately two minutes then turn the fish over. Now add the king scallops and king prawns. Cook for a further two minutes. Turn the scallops and prawns over and place the pan of fish into a hot preheated oven (220°C) for three to four minutes.

For The Samphire

Heat a little oil in a pan and lightly sauté the shallots. Add the samphire and sauté for a further minute. Add 200ml of cream and bring to a boil. Season and finish with 50g of butter, shaking the pan to incorporate the butter.

> **Chef's Tip**
>
> As the samphire is naturally salty, season with freshly ground black pepper only.

To Serve

Share the potato between four plates, top with the creamed samphire. Place the salmon and turbot on the creamed samphire then arrange two king scallops and king prawns around the base of each dish. Garnish with fresh micro herbs.

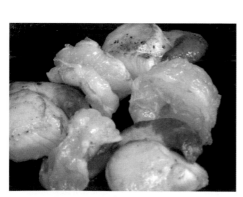

SPOTTED DICK

SERVES 5 hearty Yorkshire portions (somebody always wants seconds)

🍷 *Pineau des Charentes Blanc 10-Year-Old*
Château de Beaulon (France)

Ingredients

Spotted Dick

170g self-raising flour
salt (pinch)
85g shredded vegetarian suet
85g golden caster sugar
85g currants
$1/2$ lemon (zest of)
$1/2$ tsp mixed spice
150ml milk
4 tbsp golden syrup

Custard

575ml milk
50ml single cream
1 vanilla pod
4 egg yolks
30g caster sugar
2 level tsp cornflour

1ltr pudding basin or 5 x 150ml basins

Method

For The Spotted Dick

Sieve flour into a large mixing bowl. Add salt, suet, sugar, currants, lemon zest and mixed spices.

Add as much of the milk as is needed to form a sticky mixture. You may not need all the milk as this will depend on the absorbency of the flour.

Grease a one litre pudding basin and ladle the golden syrup across the bottom, then add the mixture.

Cover with pleated kitchen foil or greaseproof paper (the pleating allows the pudding to raise).

Steam for around one hour 45 minutes and check after one hour 30 minutes. See chef's tip. Ensure the pan does not boil dry and top up with boiling water if necessary.

If you prefer to make individual desserts, use five 150ml pudding basins or old cups, putting a dessertspoon full of golden syrup in each topped with the mixture and cover with the large basin. These should steam in about 45 minutes.

> **Chef's Tip**
>
> Check pudding is cooked by inserting a skewer into the centre. If it comes out clean it is done, if not return and steam a little longer.
>
> The vanilla pod can be washed and dried and put in a jar of caster sugar to make vanilla sugar.

For The Custard

Begin by splitting the vanilla pod lengthways and using the end of a teaspoon to scoop out the seeds.

Bring the milk, cream, vanilla pod and seeds to simmering point over a low heat. Remove the vanilla pod.

Whisk the yolks, sugar and cornflour together in a bowl until well blended.

Pour the hot milk and cream onto the eggs and sugar, whisking all the time with a balloon whisk.

Return to the pan and gently stir, over a low heat, using a wooden spatula until it thickens.

Pour the custard into a jug and serve at once. To keep hot, stand the jug in a pan of hot water and cover the top with clingfilm to prevent a skin forming.

To Serve

Turn the pudding/s out on to a plate and serve with some of the delicious homemade custard.

252
MUSE
CONTINENTAL CAFE

104B High Street, Yarm, TS15 9AU

01642 788 558
www.museyarm.com

Muse Continental Café, in the beautiful market town of Yarm, is the sister restaurant to the Michelin awarded Bay Horse in Hurworth. Serving breakfast, lunch, afternoon tea and dinner, Muse's menus comprise of classic, flavoursome dishes, served with a twist, with an emphasis on quality ingredients.

Muse has a bustling, brasserie atmosphere and boasts a licensed pavement café, giving that real Parisian feel - a great place to dine alfresco during the warmer months and to relax and watch the world go by.

Jonathan Hall and Marcus Bennett, who also own the acclaimed Bay Horse at Hurworth, felt ready for a new challenge so launched Muse with their manager from The Bay Horse, Adrian Rummel, who is the operating partner in Muse. The menu is designed by Marcus, who won the coveted title of Gastro Pub Chef of the Year and works closely with Muse's head chef, Steve Arkle.

Dishes range from steak and chips and quality burgers, to seafood pancakes, risottos and delicious salads, as well as hearty meals including lamb shank, pastas and sticky toffee pudding.

 Relish Restaurant Rewards
See page 003 for details.

The chefs at Muse have all worked very closely with Marcus Bennett and are expertly trained in high-end cuisine, often spending time in The Bay Horse's kitchen to learn the finer art of bread making and patisserie to hone their skills.

Muse was fully refurbished and launched in October 2012 by the award-winning team at the Bay Horse. The site was formerly a butcher's shop in the 1960s and during renovation, the original tiles were found and incorporated into the new design.

Modern artwork is displayed on the walls, including an E Sedgewick motif - Edie Sedgewick being 'King of Pop Art', Andy Warhol's own famous muse.

SEAFOOD PANCAKE WITH THERMIDOR SAUCE

SERVES 8

Chablis 2011 La Colombe, Burgundy (France)

Ingredients

Fish Stock

1kg fish bones (such as white turbot etc)
1 onion (peeled and chopped)
1 carrot (peeled and chopped)
1 - 2 sticks celery (chopped)
1 leek (washed and chopped)
5g butter
1 sprig parsley
1/2 ltr white wine

Thermidor Sauce

50ml white wine
2 shallots
100ml fish stock
75ml double cream
5g English mustard
20g Cheddar cheese
5g Parmesan cheese

Pancakes

200ml milk
200g eggs
200g plain flour
1kg (about 120g per person) salmon, cod and prawns (diced)

Method

For The Fish Stock

Rinse the fish bones and heads twice in cold water and remove the gills. Sweat the vegetables for two minutes. Add the bones and sweat for a further two minutes. Add the wine and cook out the alcohol. Add the parsley and one litre of cold water. Bring to a boil and simmer for 15 minutes. Strain and chill.

For The Thermidor Sauce

Place the fish stock and white wine in a pan with the shallots and reduce by two thirds. Add the cream and bring to a boil. Strain, then whisk in the English mustard, Parmesan and Cheddar cheese.

> **Chef's Tip**
> Always remove the thermidor from the stove as soon as the cream has boiled or it will separate.

For The Seafood Pancakes

Blend all of the ingredients in a liquidiser, add a pinch of salt and pass through a fine sieve. Heat a 20cm frying pan and pour in a little oil. When the oil starts to separate into pools, pour the excess off and pour in a little pancake mixture. Cover the bottom of the pan, making the pancake as thin as possible. Brown on both sides. The mixture should make eight pancakes. Place 150g of diced fish (salmon, cod, prawns, mussels) into the centre of the pancake and season with salt and pepper. Roll up the pancake and place into a microwave and cook for 20 seconds. Place each pancake in an earthenware dish, cover with the thermidor sauce and cook at 200°C for six to eight minutes or until the thermidor is bubbling.

To Serve

Serve as pictured.

PORK FILLET WRAPPED IN PARMA HAM WITH BLACK PUDDING MASH, APPLE COMPOTE & MADEIRA JUS

SERVES 4

Les Terrasses Côtes du Roussillon 2011 Domaine Boucabeille (France)

Ingredients

Pork Fillet

4 slices Parma ham
1 pork fillet (ask your butcher to remove any fat or sinew from the pork)

Apple Compote

2 apples (peeled, cored and diced)
8 tbsp orange juice
1 tbsp fresh lemon juice
20g sugar
2-3 scrapes fresh nutmeg
salt (pinch of)

Black Pudding Mash

200g potato (cooked and mashed)
50g black pudding (diced)
50ml double cream
50g unsalted butter
1 tsp salt
1 tsp white pepper

Madeira Jus

1ltr dark chicken stock
110ml Madeira
1-2 carrots (peeled and chopped)
1-2 onions (peeled and sliced)
1 clove garlic
1 sprig thyme
1-2 sticks celery (chopped)
10g sugar
10g mushrooms
15ml red wine vinegar

To Serve

spinach (cooked)
chervil
crackling

Method

For The Apple Compote

Add the apples, orange juice, lemon juice, sugar and nutmeg to a saucepan on medium-high heat. Simmer until the apples are tender and the juices have thickened to a syrup. This should take about ten to 12 minutes. Add the salt to season.

For The Black Pudding Mash

Place the cream and butter in a pan and bring to a boil. Heat the mashed potatoes in a microwave. Add the black pudding to the cream mix and whisk in the mashed potato. Season.

For The Madeira Jus

Place all the vegetables, garlic and herbs in a pan and cook, browning slightly in a little butter until soft. Add the red wine vinegar and sugar, then bring to a boil. Cook until most of the liquid has evaporated. Add 100ml of the Madeira and bring back to a boil. Reduce by half and then add the dark chicken stock. Simmer until reduced by two thirds. Strain through a fine sieve and add the remaining Madeira. Chill.

For The Pork

Lay out three sheets of clingfilm to approximately the length of the pork. Lay the Parma ham on top of the clingfilm and top with the pork fillet. Roll the pork in the Parma ham, then in the clingfilm. Tighten and tie at both ends. Leave to set in the fridge for one hour. Remove from the fridge and cut into four portions. Remove the clingfilm and brown on all sides in a frying pan. Place in an oven preheated to 180°C and cook for 12 minutes. Leave to rest for five minutes.

To Serve

Warm the black pudding mash in a pan and heat the Madeira jus. Place the black pudding mash to one side of the plate. Place a small mound of spinach to the other and top with the pork and crackling. Place a blob of apple compote on the plate and drizzle with the jus. Garnish with chervil.

CHOCOLATE BROWNIE WITH CHOCOLATE SAUCE, MINT CHOC CHIP ICE CREAM & CHANTILLY CREAM

SERVES 8

Noble Late Harvest Sauvignon 2008 Mulderbosch (South Africa)

Ingredients

Chocolate Sauce

2 egg yolks
25g caster sugar
125ml cream (warmed)
50g milk chocolate

Brownies

450g caster sugar
6 eggs
337g butter
125g cocoa
125g flour
337g dark chocolate
150g white chocolate

20cm x 20cm baking tray/cake tin

Chantilly Cream

250ml double cream
25g icing sugar
1-2 vanilla pods (split)
2 drops vanilla extract

Mint Ice Cream

150g dark chocolate (crushed)
1 tsp mint essence
2 tsp green food colouring
200ml cream
300ml milk
5 egg yolks
75g sugar
1 tbsp glucose
15g butter

Garnish

mint leaves
cocoa powder

Method

For The Chocolate Sauce

Whisk the egg yolks and slowly add the sugar. Warm the cream and add to the eggs. Add the chocolate and whisk to a custard consistency.

For The Brownies

Melt the chocolate with the butter and cool. Beat the eggs and sugar until thick, then fold in the chocolate mix. Mix the dry ingredients and add to the chocolate mixture. Pour into a lined, 20cm square dish and bake for 40 minutes on 170°C. Remove from the oven and cut into eight.

For The Chantilly Cream

Place the cream, icing sugar and vanilla extract in a bowl and whisk to form soft peaks. Scrape the seeds from the vanilla pods and add to the cream mixture.

For The Ice Cream

Bring the milk and cream to a boil in a pan with the butter, then whisk in the glucose. Whisk the egg yolks with the sugar until pale and creamy. Pour the milk and cream over the egg and sugar mix and whisk over a low heat until the mixture reaches 82°C. Whisking all the time, pass through a fine sieve.

When the ice cream is cold, fold in the chocolate, mint essence and food colouring. Churn in an ice cream machine.

To Serve

Place the warm brownie on the plate and put the ice cream to one side. Serve with a swipe of the chocolate sauce and a blob of the Chantilly cream. Sprinkle with cocoa powder and garnish with a mint leaf.

262
NINETEEN RESTAURANT

19 Grape Lane, York, YO1 7HU

01904 636 366
www.nineteenyork.com

Head chef and proprietor Matt Beevers was born in the beautiful Yorkshire seaside gem of Robin Hood's Bay, where his love of cooking and food began at an early age.

"After college my love for food and hospitality led me to France. I travelled between the south west coast and the magnificent Alps, from five star luxury chalet hotels to busy seafood brasseries, all the while building on my passion for fresh, exciting food. I moved home to the Yorkshire coast three years ago to combine the classic French techniques I had learned with the fabulous produce available to me here.

"If asked to describe my style of food I would simply answer, I take beautiful produce, cook them with respect and garnish with imagination."

Nineteen Restaurant overlooks the cobbles of one of York's oldest streets. Beautiful exposed beams married with a simple elegant décor provide the setting for you to graze at leisure whilst watching the bustling world go by.

"When I bought Nineteen in February 2012, it was love at first sight. I was looking for a place to provide a relaxed dining experience and to truly showcase my passion for food and wine. I found it here."

Relish Restaurant Rewards
See page 003 for details.

COFFEE YARD
FORMERLY
LANGTON LANE

LEADING TO STONEGATE

Both myself and my sous chef Chris Grant (York's Young Chef of the Year 2009) have a real passion for working with the greatest of local producers and suppliers, from our meat direct from the Dales to our top class east coast landed fish and seafood. Chris's love for the new wave of molecular gastronomy combined with my passion and respect for the classics creates an interesting and imaginative range of menus, from a traditional Sunday Roast to our elaborate tasting menu where we really go to town.

PAN SEARED SCALLOPS, PIG'S CHEEK & YORKSHIRE RHUBARB

SERVES 4

🍷 *Pouilly Fuissé, Domaine Saumaize-Michelin 2011 (France)*

Ingredients

Scallops

12 medium diver-caught scallops (cleaned and coral removed)
flaked sea salt
oil (for frying)

Braised Pig's Cheeks

3 pig's cheeks (trimmed)
1 carrot
1 white onion
1 stick celery
1 sprig fresh thyme
1 clove garlic
500ml beef stock
250ml bold red wine
50g chives (finely chopped)

Sour Rhubarb Sticks

30cm piece rhubarb (cut neatly into 12 x 2.5cm pieces)
1 lemon (juice of)
salt (pinch of)
5g caster sugar
50ml water

Sweet Rhubarb Coulis

30cm piece of rhubarb (finely chopped)
15g caster sugar
10ml water

Garnish

micro basil

Method

For The Braised Pig's Cheek And Jus

Preheat the oven to 160°C.

Using an ovenproof pan, heat a little oil and brown the cheeks then set them aside. Add the chopped onion, celery and carrot to the pot and cook for a couple of minutes to colour. Put the cheeks back in with the vegetables and add the stock, wine, thyme and garlic and simmer for five minutes.

Cover the pot and put in the oven for two and a half to three hours, until the cheeks are tender. Remove the cheeks and shred them into a clean mixing bowl. Season to taste and add the chopped chives.

On a large sheet of clingfilm, arrange the shredded cheeks into a sausage shape about 2.5cm diameter and roll tightly. Refrigerate until ready to serve.

Strain the braising stock into a pan and reduce to 75ml, skimming any fat from the surface as you go. Season and keep warm.

For The Sour Rhubarb Sticks

Mix the lemon juice, water, salt and sugar in a saucepan.

Add the rhubarb sticks and bring to boiling point. As soon as they reach the boil, remove the rhubarb and pat dry using kitchen towel. Keep warm.

For The Sweet Rhubarb Coulis

Add all the ingredients into a saucepan and set over a low heat. Cook gently until the rhubarb is tender.

Remove from the heat and blitz in a food processor, pass through a fine sieve and keep warm.

To Serve

Season the scallops. Heat a little oil in a large frying pan and sear the seasoned scallops for two minutes, then flip gently and cook for a further minute. Remove and keep warm. Slice the pig's cheek into 12 even slices and brown each side in the scallop pan. Remove and keep warm. In the same pan, warm through the rhubarb batons.

To plate the dish start by swiping the coulis down the centre, arrange three scallops and three slices of cheek alternately along the coulis. Top each scallop with a piece of rhubarb and drizzle with the jus. Finish with a couple of sprigs of micro basil and serve.

> **Chef's Tip**
>
> I don't like to serve the orange coral of the scallops on this dish, however don't throw them away! Dry them out in the oven, season and blitz into a powder then mix into softened butter for an amazing flavoured butter to serve with steak.

MONKFISH WITH WILD MUSHROOM ARANCINI, TOMATO & YORKSHIRE CHORIZO

SERVES 4

Rully Blanc Cuvée St Jaques Albert Sounit 2008 (France)

Ingredients

Monkfish
800g monkfish tail (cut into 4 portions)
8 thin slices Parma ham

Arancini
100g risotto rice (Arborio)
1 medium banana shallot (finely chopped)
1 clove garlic (finely chopped)
200g mixed wild mushrooms (sliced, brushed clean, not washed)
300ml hot chicken or vegetable stock
1 tsp rapeseed oil
50g chives (finely chopped)
1 egg (beaten with a splash of water)
flour and breadcrumbs (to coat)
flaked sea salt
oil (for deep frying)

Tomato Sauce
500g ripe vine tomatoes
1 large onion
1 clove garlic
50ml red wine vinegar
50ml white wine
50g caster sugar
1 tsp rapeseed oil
seasoning

Garnish
100g ring Yorkshire chorizo (or Spanish if you can't find Yorkshire)
4 small bunches cherry tomatoes on the vine
few sprigs lamb's leaf

Method

For The Monkfish

On a large square of clingfilm, place two pieces of Parma ham next to each other slightly overlapping. Lay a piece of monkfish over the ham and roll tightly, repeat with the other three pieces. Tie the ends of the clingfilm to create a tight well sealed *boudin*. In a large pan of boiling water poach the monkfish for five minutes.

> **Chef's Tip**
> Monkfish is an amazing meaty fish, however not the easiest to prepare so ask your fishmonger to do it for you!

For The Arancini

In a large heavy pan, heat the rapeseed oil and gently sauté the finely chopped shallot, chives, garlic and mushrooms. When the onions start to soften, add the rice and stir to coat the rice in the oil. Slowly add the chicken stock in small amounts, allowing all the liquid to be absorbed before adding more. When all the liquid is absorbed the mixture should be quite dry and not sloppy. The rice should be cooked but not mushy. Spread over a baking sheet and chill in the fridge until cool enough to handle. Once cool, divide into four and roll into balls. Roll in the flour, then egg, then breadcrumbs, then egg, then breadcrumbs again. Fry until golden. Keep warm.

For The Tomato Sauce

In a saucepan, heat the oil and add the onion, garlic and tomatoes (all roughly chopped) and allow to cook slowly until the onions and tomatoes are soft and start to break up. Turn up the heat and add the vinegar, wine and sugar, then simmer for about ten minutes. Pour everything into a food processor and blend until smooth. Season to taste and keep warm.

To Serve

Preheat oven to 200°C.

Carefully remove the clingfilm from the monkfish, pat dry and panfry until golden all the way round. Slice the chorizo on an angle and arrange in four rows on a baking sheet. Place a piece of monkfish on each row of chorizo, put the cherry tomatoes on the same tray and drizzle with a little oil and seasoning. Bake for ten minutes.

Spoon the hot tomato sauce onto your chosen plates and arrange the monkfish, sliced into three, on top. Sit a risotto ball to the side. Arrange the chorizo slices around the plate with the cherry tomatoes, then finally drizzle with the bright red oil from the roasting tray and garnish with a few sprigs of lamb's leaf.

SUMMER GARDEN AFTERNOON TEA

SERVES 4

🍷 *Eiswein Pinot Noir, Hopler 2009*
(Austria)

Ingredients

Earl Grey Panna Cotta

200ml double cream
200ml full fat milk
3 Earl Grey tea bags
75g caster sugar
2$\frac{1}{2}$ leaves gelatine (soaked)

Scones

115g self-raising flour
25g butter (at room temperature)
15g sugar
75ml milk
salt (pinch of)

Bergamot Sorbet

250ml water
150g caster sugar
2 Yorkshire tea bags
20g glucose
bergamot essence to taste
1 lemon (juice of)

Honey Jelly

150g clear honey
150ml water
2$\frac{1}{2}$ leaves gelatine (soaked)

Strawberry Gel

400g strawberries
50g caster sugar
1g agar agar

Chantilly Cream

200ml double cream
75g caster sugar
$\frac{1}{2}$ vanilla pod (seeds scraped out)

Garnish

fresh strawberries (cut into quarters)

4 vintage tea cups

Method

For The Bergamot Sorbet

Add all the ingredients to a heavy pan and bring to a boil. Allow to cool then remove the tea bags. Churn in an ice cream maker.

For The Scones

Preheat oven to 220°C. Rub together the flour, butter, salt and sugar. Add milk to form a soft dough. Roll out on a floured surface to 2cm thick. Cut out using a 3cm scone cutter, glaze with a little milk and bake for 12 minutes. Remove from the oven and allow to cool.

For The Panna Cotta

Simmer the cream, milk, sugar and tea for three minutes. Remove tea bags and whisk in the soaked gelatine. Bring to a boil. Allow to cool then divide into four vintage tea cups and set in the fridge for two to three hours prior to serving.

For The Strawberry Gel

Bring all ingredients to a simmer. Cook for three minutes then blitz until smooth. Allow to cool. Blitz again before serving.

For The Honey Jelly

Bring the water and honey to a simmer, add the soaked gelatine then bring to a boil. Pour into a small baking tin to set. Once set, cut into cubes and roll in sugar (they should look like little sugar cubes).

For The Chantilly Cream

Whisk all ingredients until thick enough to hold its shape. Chill until needed.

To Serve

Crumble a mini scone down the centre of each plate and build a little pile at one end to seat your sorbet. Position the tea cup of panna cotta, build a mini jam and cream scone (with the Chantilly cream and strawberry gel) then place opposite the tea cup. Scoop a ball of sorbet and place on the crumbled scone. Decorate the plate with cubes of the honey jelly, neat dots of the strawberry gel, a scoop of the Chantilly cream and finish with a couple of strawberry quarters.

Chef's Tip

With the presentation of this, dish let your imagination run wild.

272
THE ROSE & CROWN

The Rose & Crown at Romaldkirk, Barnard Castle, Co Durham, DL12 9EB

01833 650 213
www.rose-and-crown.co.uk

The Rose & Crown is a quintessential English coaching inn dating back to the 18th Century. While keeping up with the times in many respects, it still retains all of those delightful things that we associate with the great British inn. Big stone fireplaces, beamed ceilings, polished brass and nick-nacks, reflecting the rural heritage of the dale, adorn the walls. Everything about the Rose & Crown is immediately welcoming and cosy with service to match. It is an added bonus that it just happens to stand on the village green of Romaldkirk, a picture postcard village in the beautiful countryside of Teesdale, just a few miles up-river from the market town of Barnard Castle.

The Rose & Crown offers two different dining options. A more informal experience can be enjoyed in the relaxing surroundings of the bar and brasserie, where a daily lunch and supper menu is served. If you are in the mood for something a bit 'posher', the two AA rosette awarded restaurant provides the perfect rural fine dining setting. Oak panelled walls, polished silver and crisp white napkins set the tone for that special occasion, not that you need an excuse. Dinner is served daily and lunch on Sundays.

With 12 beautifully appointed bedrooms, there is the opportunity to make a complete night of it. After dinner, settle into a comfortable wingback chair by the fire with a glass of port, a brandy or perhaps a malt whisky. Decisions, decisions...

 Relish Restaurant Rewards
See page 003 for details.

The surrounding dales provide fantastic produce and the chefs work closely with local suppliers. The Robinsons, who own the Rose & Crown, are a farming family so they understand the importance of this relationship. These beautiful ingredients are then used by Henny Crosland and her kitchen team to create dishes that give a nod to traditional British and French cuisine but with a modern approach to both excite the palate and the eye. First it's got to look great and then it's got to taste even better!

WOOD PIGEON & BLACK PUDDING WITH PORT GLAZE

SERVES 4

 Chianti 2010, Vignosi (Tuscany, Italy)

Ingredients

8 wood pigeon breasts

Black Pudding

100g black pudding
4 slices pancetta

Port Glaze

1 onion
1 sprig fresh thyme (chopped)
300ml port
200ml chicken stock
1 tbsp redcurrant jelly

Garnish

herb flowers

Method

For The Port Glaze

Finely chop the onion and then gently fry until translucent. Add the chopped thyme and port. Reduce until only half the original volume is left. Add the redcurrant jelly and the chicken stock. Reduce down to one quarter of the volume; you should be left with a syrupy consistency.

For The Black Pudding

Cut the black pudding into eight cylinders and wrap in the pancetta. Season the cylinders and fry. Once cooked, place to one side.

For The Wood Pigeon

Season the breasts and fry for one minute on each side. Remove from the pan and rest for three to five minutes.

> **Chef's Tip**
> Pigeon is best served pink so be careful not to over cook, resting is the key to success.

To Serve

Brush a stripe of port glaze in the centre of the plate. Arrange two cylinders of black pudding on to the stripe. Take the rested pigeon breast and cut in half, arrange between the black pudding. Garnish with herb flowers.

TROUT WITH RAZOR CLAM, FENNEL PUREE & A WATERCRESS FOAM

SERVES 4

Macon Uchizy 2011, Talmard
(Burgundy, France)

Ingredients

Fish

4 trout fillets
4 razor clams (cleaned and cooked - retain the shells to serve)
100g samphire
100g sea vegetables
knob of butter

Watercress Foam

1 pack watercress
1 onion
50g spinach
50ml milk
100ml fish stock

Fennel Purée

1 onion
2 heads fennel
100ml fish stock (hot)

Garnish

wild garlic flowers

Method

For The Fennel Purée

Finely chop the onion and fennel heads and fry until translucent. Add 100ml of fish stock and bring to a boil. Reduce until you are left with three quarters of your original volume. Blend and pass through a sieve.

For The Watercress Foam

Roughly chop the onion and fry until translucent. Add 100ml of fish stock. Bring to a boil and add the watercress and spinach. Boil for one minute then drain, retaining the cooking stock. Blend the spinach and watercress, adding the stock as you go, until you have a thick mixture. Keep blending and add the milk until you are left with a soup-like consistency.

For The Fish

Cut each trout fillet in half. Cut each razor clam into 1cm strips. Fry the samphire and sea vegetables with a knob of butter. Cook until warmed through. Fry the trout fillets for two minutes on each side. Set the pan aside and add the cooked clams to warm through.

> **Chef's Tip**
> Ask your fishmonger to clean and prepare your razor clams for you.

To Serve

Arrange the sea vegetables and samphire on the fennel purée. Place the trout on top of the vegetables. Put the clam pieces back into the shell and place on top of the trout. Using a hand blender, whisk the watercress mixture, scoop off the foam, add to the dish and serve. Garnish with wild garlic flowers.

CHOCOLATE TART

SERVES 8

*Campbells Rutherglen Muscat N.V.
(Australia)*

Ingredients

Sweet Pastry

225g plain flour
1 lemon (zest of)
150g butter
75g caster sugar
1 egg yolk
1 egg

Chocolate Filling

300g dark chocolate
80g butter
240ml cream
75ml milk
salt (pinch of)

White Chocolate Mousse

170g white chocolate
375ml double cream
crushed pistachio nuts (to coat end of cylinder)
100g dark chocolate (melted, to make cylinder)
acetate sheet

Garnish

gold leaf
8 chocolate truffles
strawberry flowers

Method

For The Sweet Pastry

Rub the butter into the flour. Add the sugar and lemon zest and mix together. Add all the egg and mix again. Shape into a ball and rest in the fridge for one hour.

Roll out and place in a 15cm loose bottom flan ring. *Blind bake* for eight minutes at 180°C. Remove beans and bake for a further two minutes. Allow to cool.

For The Chocolate Filling

Heat the cream. Pour the heated cream over the chocolate and butter. Mix until it melts. Add the milk and salt and pour into the pastry case. Leave to set for one hour in the fridge.

For The White Chocolate Mousse

Melt the chocolate over a *bain-marie*. Whip the cream until it forms soft peaks. Add the warm chocolate to the cream. Stir until combined. Set in a piping bag. Leave to set for one hour in the fridge.

For The Chocolate Cylinder

Paint a line of melted chocolate onto an acetate sheet. Roll the sheet into a cylinder with the chocolate line on the inside. Join the acetate together to hold the cylinder. Leave to set in the fridge for two hours. Remove the acetate and you will have a chocolate cylinder.

Pipe the white chocolate mousse into the cylinder. Dip the ends into finely crushed pistachio nuts.

To Serve

Assemble the elements on the plate as shown in the picture. Decorate with gold leaf and strawberry flowers and a chocolate truffle.

Chef's Tip

Cut the tart with a hot, dry knife for a perfect slice.

282
SAMUEL'S RESTAURANT

Swinton Park, Masham, Ripon, North Yorkshire, HG4 4JH

01765 680 900
www.swintonpark.com

Swinton Park is the ancestral home of the Earl of Swinton, owned and run by the Cunliffe-Lister family. Set in 200 acres of parkland on the edge of the Yorkshire Dales, the castle combines the style and elegance of a stately home with the comfort and exemplary service of a luxury hotel. There are 31 individually designed bedrooms - including five suites, lavishly furnished public rooms with chandeliers and ornate fireplaces, and a relaxing spa with a cedar hot tub, sauna and five treatment rooms.

The hotel's location, within a 20,000 acre estate on the edge of the Yorkshire Dales, makes its offering truly unique. The Swinton Estate (also in the ownership of the Cunliffe-Lister family) not only provides the setting for a wide range of outdoor activities including golf, falconry, shooting, fishing, cycling, walking and horse riding, but it is also the source of much of the produce used in the restaurant and cookery school. Game birds, venison and foraged ingredients, such as elderflower, wild garlic and wild mushrooms, come from the estate while, closer to the hotel, a four acre walled garden provides home-grown produce throughout most of the year.

Swinton Park's fine dining restaurant, Samuels, is located in the dining room of the castle. It is called Samuel's after Samuel Cunliffe-Lister, who built the dining room wing in 1890, following his purchase of Swinton Park in 1880. It boasts an ornate gold leaf ceiling and sweeping views of the parkland that contribute to a memorable dining experience. Guided by the experienced hand of Simon Crannage, head chef since 2007, the style of cuisine is modern British, focusing on seasonal, local produce with a serious commitment to a 'gate to plate', low food miles philosophy. The freshness and quality of the ingredients speak for themselves, with Samuel's winning a host of awards - most recently the Visit England 'Taste of England' gold award for 2013.

Situated just off the A1(M), mid-way way between London and Edinburgh and close to the historic cities of York, Leeds and Harrogate, Swinton Park is easily accessed from most of the UK making it the perfect location for a day out or short break.

Relish Restaurant Rewards
See page 003 for details.

Recent accolades for Samuel's include listings in Harden's Guide with an 'exceptional' for ambiance, three AA Rosettes, Trip Advisor Travellers Choice Award 2013 as a Top 10 UK hotel and Visit England Taste of England Gold Award 2013.

'TODAY'S GARDEN PRODUCE' WITH LOWNA DAIRY HALDENBY BLUE CREAM

SERVES 4

🍷 *Gentil, Hugel, Alsace, 2011*
(France)

Ingredients

Vegetables

4 baby carrots
4 baby turnip
4 fresh asparagus
4 fresh young radish
4 spring onions

Haldenby Cream

(Haldenby Blue is a multi gold award-winning cheese from Lowna Dairy in the east of Yorkshire)

1 whole Haldenby Blue cheese (rind on)
100ml water
100g cream
4 leaves gelatine

Method

At the castle we are very fortunate to have a large working kitchen garden. If you grow your own vegetables, leaves and herbs - great. If not, use a local deli or grocers.

We use young, tasty baby vegetables and herbs for this dish, but it is up to you what you use, just make sure it is crisp and fresh!

For The Vegetables

Clean and trim the vegetables.

For The Haldenby Blue Cream

Bloom the gelatine in ice water and set aside. Heat the water and cream to a simmer. Place the Haldenby cheese in a food blender with the cream and water mixture and blend until smooth. Add the soaked gelatine. Once the gelatine has dissolved, pass through a sieve and set in a bowl with clingfilm on top. Once set, whip the mousse with a hand whisk and place into a serving bowl.

This can be made in advance but make sure it comes out of the fridge in plenty of time to warm up a little.

To Serve

Serve the cheese sauce at room temperature with the raw vegetables.

ESTATE VENISON, SALT BAKED BEETROOT, CELERIAC, HONEY BAKED OATS

SERVES 4

🍷 *Herdade de Sao Miguel, Colheita Seleccionada, Alentejano, 2011 (Portugal)*

Ingredients

Venison

1 venison loin (trimmed and cut into 4)
1 clove garlic
1 sprig thyme
50ml olive oil
75g unsalted butter
Maldon sea salt
cracked black pepper

Celeriac Purée

1 small celeriac (peeled and chopped)
250ml whole milk
250ml double cream
1 star anise
50g unsalted butter
table salt
1/2 lemon (juice of)

Venison Jus

1 kg venison bones*
1 stick celery (finely chopped)
1/2 leek (finely chopped)
1 clove garlic
200ml red wine (good quality)
150ml ruby port
2 juniper berries
1 sprig thyme
1ltr veal stock**
2 strips orange zest

*venison bones are available from most quality local butchers
**veal stock is available from most delis and larger supermarkets

Salt Baked Beetroot

4 medium sized purple beetroot
Maldon sea salt
75ml olive oil

Honey Baked Oats

200g porridge oats
75g butter
75g honey

Method

For The Venison

Season the venison with the Maldon sea salt and cracked black pepper. Place a large frying pan on a high heat with the olive oil. Add the venison and seal for one to two minutes on both sides. Once sealed, add the thyme, garlic and butter and roast in a preheated oven for five to six minutes at 180°C. Once the venison is cooked, remove from the oven and the pan and allow to rest for eight to ten minutes (resting the venison will allow the meat to become tender). Keep to one side until ready to serve.

For The Celeriac Purée

Place the celeriac in a heavy bottomed pan with the milk, cream and star anise. Slowly bring the pan to a boil. Once it has reached boiling point, reduce to a simmer and cook until the celeriac is very soft (this should take around 12 to 15 minutes). When the celeriac is cooked, remove the star anise and strain off the liquid (but reserve the liquid to adjust the consistency of the purée later on). Place the cooked celeriac and butter in a food processor and blend on full power for three to five minutes until the celeriac is smooth, adjusting the purée with the reserved liquid to reach the desired consistency. Season with the lemon juice and salt to taste.

For The Jus

In a pan, sweat the celery, leek and garlic with colour. Add the alcohol and boil for one minute. Then add the stock, juniper berries, bones, thyme and the orange zest. Bring to a boil and simmer for 40 minutes. Strain into a clean pan and reduce until you reach the desired consistency. Pass through a fine sieve. (This sauce can be made in advance and stored in the fridge for up to one week).

For The Beetroot

Wash and scrub the beetroot to remove all of the dirt. Season well with Maldon sea salt and the olive oil. Wrap each beetroot twice with aluminium foil and place on a baking tray. Bake in a preheated oven for 45 to 60 minutes at 160°C. Remove from the oven and allow to cool for 20 minutes in the foil. Remove the foil and, while still warm, rub off the skin with your thumbs (you may wish to use food safe gloves as this may stain your hands). Cut the beetroot into six equal segments and serve.

For The Oats

Warm the honey and butter together, pour over the oats and mix well. Place on non-stick tray and bake in the oven at 170°C for five to ten minutes or until golden. You may need to mix the oats from time to time while baking to stop them from sticking together. Allow to cool and crisp before serving.

To Serve

Assemble on the plate as pictured.

STRAWBERRY, VERBENA & PISTACHIO

SERVES 4

🍷 *Coteaux du Layon, Châeau La Variere, 2007
(France)*

Ingredients

Strawberry Coulis

(for use in two recipes below)

500g strawberries (hulled)
175g caster sugar
1 lemon (juice of)

Macerated Strawberries

12 strawberries (hulled)
100g strawberry coulis
100g water
75g sugar
2 drops vanilla essence

Verbena Sorbet

180g sugar
100g glucose syrup*
500g water
200ml lemon juice
400g fresh leaves lemon verbena**

Pistachio Meringue

4 egg whites
100g sugar
75g pistachios

Garnish

4 fresh strawberries (cut into quarters)
20 verbena leaves

*glucose syrup is widely available in most supermarkets
**lemon verbena is available from selected greengrocers

Method

For The Strawberry Coulis

Place all the ingredients in a food processor and blend until smooth. Pass through a fine sieve and reserve until required.

For The Macerated Strawberries

Place the coulis, water, sugar and vanilla essence in a pan and warm until the sugar dissolves. Remove from the heat and allow to cool. Put the hulled strawberries into a bowl and cover with the coulis mixture. Clingfilm the bowl and allow to macerate in the fridge for four hours before serving.

For The Strawberry Leather

Spread a thin layer of the strawberry coulis on a sheet of silicone paper. Set the oven to the lowest possible setting and place the sheet in the oven overnight to allow the coulis to dry out. Remove the sheet of coulis from the silicone paper while it is still warm. Cut to your desired shape to serve.

For The Verbena Sorbet (Prepare up to three days in advance)

Place the sugar, glucose, water and lemon juice in a heavy bottomed pan and slowly bring it up to 87°C. Add the verbena leaves, remove from the heat and allow the verbena to infuse for up to two days. If you have an ice cream machine then churn the sorbet for 20 to 30 minutes and reserve in the freezer. If you do not have an ice cream machine, place the sorbet in a freeze-safe bowl, place in the freezer and stir the sorbet every hour until it has fully set.

For The Pistachio Meringue (Prepare up to two days in advance)

Place the egg whites in a large bowl and whisk with an electric whisk. When the egg whites reach the ribbon stage, (which is when you can see the whisk leaving tracks in the egg whites), slowly add the sugar until it is all incorporated. Keep whisking until the egg whites are shiny and form stiff peaks (you should be able to hold the bowl above your head without the meringue falling out). Spread the meringue in a thin layer onto silicone paper. Roughly chop the pistachio nuts and sprinkle onto the meringue. Set the oven to the lowest possible setting and place the sheet of meringue in the oven overnight to allow it to dry out. Snap pieces off as you need them.

To Serve

Assemble on the plate as pictured.

292
SWINTON PARK COOKERY SCHOOL

Swinton Park, Masham, Ripon, North Yorkshire, HG4 4JH

01765 680 969
www.swintonpark.com

The Cookery School at Swinton Park has been running since 2003 and has consistently achieved high acclaim, most recently as a finalist in British Cookery School Awards 2012. Located on the ground floor of the Georgian stable wing adjacent to Swinton Park hotel, the teaching kitchen is a light and airy room, furnished in country-kitchen style and fitted with the latest appliances and equipment.

The cookery school also benefits from the hotel's location at the heart of the Swinton Estate, with much of the produce used in the school coming from the parkland and walled garden.

Stephen Bulmer joined the cookery school as chef director in January 2013. He is also widely acknowledged to be one the leading cookery school tutors in the UK, having been chef director of the Raymond Blanc Cookery School for six years and also running his own cookery school at Brook Hall in Buckinghamshire. He combines his top-level cookery skills with a gregarious personality - a winning combination. "He is one of my most experienced chefs and a great craftsman - his enthusiasm is completely infectious," commented Raymond Blanc.

Whilst his career has taken him to work at Michelin starred restaurants all over the world, Stephen hails from Yorkshire and so has returned to his roots. He spent his childhood in a village on the North Yorkshire Moors, with his first cooking job at The Goathland Hotel, before going on to train at The Box Tree in Ilkley.

Stephen has created a new schedule of half day, one day and two day courses at Swinton Park which are open to residents and non-residents of all levels of ability. Courses cover a wide range of cuisines and techniques, with themes ranging from Flavours of the Orient to Regional French Cuisine, Barbecue Cookery to Delicious Desserts and Tapas to Bread Making. There are also courses for children, teenagers and professional chefs. Guest chefs teaching occasional classes include celebrity chef Rosemary Shrager and a number of other specialists running courses such as Wild About Food (foraging for wild edible ingredients) and a regular Curry Club.

The cookery school provides a relaxed, informal setting for Chef's Table demonstration dining evenings, where Stephen prepares and serves a gourmet meal in front of you. The school is also available for private hire and for corporate, incentive and team-building events.

Relish Restaurant Rewards
See page 003 for details.

294
SHIBDEN MILL INN

Shibden Mill Fold, Shibden, Halifax, West Yorkshire, HX3 7UL

01422 365 840
www.shibdenmillinn.com

Shibden Mill nestles in the fold of West Yorkshire's Shibden Valley, where it is surrounded by rolling countryside, an idyllic setting for this 17th Century four star inn. Owners Simon and Caitlin Heaton have sensitively restored the historic property, which now presents 11 individually styled, stunning guest rooms; a cosy bar and dining area, with low beamed ceilings and open fires; an upstairs restaurant and private dining. The Inn's reputation for fabulous food and warm hospitality extends far beyond the Yorkshire borders and Shibden Mill has been awarded two AA rosettes.

Heading up things in the kitchen is Darren Parkinson, a dynamic young man with an eye for excellence and innovative food combinations. The culinary team attracts widespread acclaim for shaping dishes rich with inspiration, quality and diversity. Working with the seasons forms the basis of a menu that presents the very best of whatever is being harvested at the time, with ingredients sourced locally to showcase the region's finest fish, poultry, game, meat, vegetables and fruit. A wonderful selection of Cask Marque approved ales, including the Shibden Mill's own brew, and an extensive wine list complement proceedings. This splendid inn never fails to impress and is firmly positioned on the region's culinary map. The whole experience of dining and staying here makes planning your next visit a topic of conversation before you have even left.

 Relish Restaurant Rewards
See page 003 for details.

The Inn's reputation for warm hospitality, premier gastro dining and first class accommodation draws people to the Shibden Valley from far and wide. For those stopping over in one of Shibden Mill's 11 luxurious guest rooms, there is much to explore. The beautiful surroundings of this elegant 17th Century property make it very easy to just relax and unwind. For those simply wishing to 'down tools' and indulge, once you have arrived and unpacked, there's no reason to leave.

CONFIT BELLY OF SHIBDEN VALLEY PIG, CRISPY LOBSTER, PASSION FRUIT, DRIED CHILLI & CORIANDER

SERVES 6

Gewürztraminerr: Mittlewihr, Alsace Philippe Gocker (France) or Colombard & Gros Manseng: Côtes de Gascogne, Domaine de Miselle (France)

Ingredients

Confit Pork Belly

500g pork belly
duck fat (enough to cover)
5 garlic cloves
bay leaves
thyme
5g pink peppercorns (crushed)
20g coarse sea salt

Lobster

1 x 1lb lobster
1 whole lemon
5 garlic cloves
bay leaves

Batter

100g flour
100g cornflour
sparkling water

Passion Fruit Purée

10 passion fruits
500ml water
200g sugar

Garnish

1 fresh chilli
coriander

Method

For The Pork Belly

Salt the pork belly for a couple of hours at room temperature by rubbing the salt and crushed peppercorns into both sides of the pork. Leave for two hours, then wash the salt off in cold water and dry with a clean cloth.

Put the belly in a pan or casserole pot and cover with the duck fat. Add the rest of the ingredients and cook for two to three hours at 120°C. Chill in the fridge after cooking.

For The Lobster

Bring a pan of cold water to a boil and add all the ingredients. Simmer for ten minutes, then bring back to a boil. Cook the lobster for one more minute then put straight into an ice bath to cool. After cooking, place the lobster to one side for later.

For The Passion Fruit

Halve the passion fruits with a sharp knife and scoop the seeds out with a small spoon. Put in a pan, add the water, reduce by half, then add the sugar and simmer for ten minutes. Leave to cool down.

For The Chilli

Start by halving the chilli and removing the seeds. Cut into long thin strips, or *julienne*. Place on a non-stick tray and dry out in the oven at 100°C for about one hour.

To Finish

Portion the belly into small square pieces and reheat in a hot pan, skin side down for eight minutes in the oven. Make a batter with the flour and cornflour by adding the sparkling water little by little to form a thin batter. Remove the lobster from the shell, cut the meat into 30g pieces and coat in the batter. Fry the lobster last minute in a frying pan.

To Serve

Place the belly pork and lobster in the middle of the plate. Spoon the passion fruit around the plate and scatter the chilli and the coriander on top of the lobster.

POACHED & ROASTED CALDERDALE RABBIT, PEA PUREE, WILD GARLIC, GARDEN RADISHES & GAME JUS

SERVES 6

Viognier: Languedoc Domaine de Vedilhan (France) or Sangiovese di Puglia: 'Laroma' Castel Boglione, (Italy)

Ingredients

Rabbit

2 rabbit saddles
wild garlic (chopped)
thyme (chopped)
1 clove garlic (crushed)
20g butter
air dried ham (4 thin slices)

Pea Purée

500g fresh or frozen peas
200ml chicken stock
1 clove garlic

Garnish

baby radishes
pea shoots
wild garlic leaves
rack of rabbit (optional)
game jus (optional)

Method

For The Rabbit

De-bone the saddles of rabbit leaving you with four loins. Place the ham on a clean, flat surface. Roll the rabbit loins in the wild garlic and thyme, then roll up in the ham, wrap in clingfilm and poach in boiling water for three minutes.

For The Pea Purée

Bring the chicken stock to a boil, with the clove of garlic. Add the peas and cook for two minutes. Put straight into a food processor and blend to a smooth paste. Add water if need be, season and leave to cool.

To Finish

Take the rabbit loins out of the clingfilm and fry in a medium to hot pan with the garlic and butter. Roast in the oven at 180°C for three to four minutes.

To Serve

Cut the loins in half and place on the plate, along with the pea purée. Garnish with some halved baby radishes, pea shoots and wild garlic leaves. Finish with a drizzle of game jus.

PISTACHIO & MARSHMALLOW SOUFFLE, MACAROONS & DARK CHOCOLATE SAUCE

SERVES 6

 Moscato: Pantelleria 'Passito di Pantelleria'
Pellegrino (Italy)

Method

For The Soufflé

First make the soufflé base by boiling the milk with the pistachio paste. Add a couple of tablespoons of water to the cornflour and add to the milk mix. Whisk till the mixture is thick, leave to cool.

Line the ramekins with butter and caster sugar by brushing melted butter around the inside of the ramekin then coating with sugar. Whisk the egg whites until they form stiff peaks. Add the caster sugar little by little until firm. Fold the whites into the pistachio soufflé base and spoon into the ramekins. Bake the soufflés at 190°C for 13 to 14 minutes.

For The Macaroons

Whisk the egg white and the caster sugar for about five minutes. Use a food processor to blend the icing sugar, ground almonds and colouring. With a large spoon, fold the almond mixture into the egg white, then beat with the spoon until the mixture is half the volume you started with. Pipe the macaroon mix onto parchment paper (in small rounds) and leave to stand for ten minutes. Cook for 15 minutes at 160°C.

For The Chocolate Sauce

Simply melt the chocolate and the milk together in a saucepan and set aside.

To Serve

Serve the soufflé with the macaroons and chocolate sauce.

Ingredients

Soufflé

500ml milk
40g cornflour
15g pistachio paste
175g egg whites
100g caster sugar
10g butter (melted)

Macaroons

30g ground almonds
60g icing sugar
yellow food colouring
1 egg white
10g caster sugar

Dark Chocolate Sauce

100g dark chocolate
200ml milk

6 x 5oz ramekins

THE TALBOT HOTEL

Yorkersgate, Malton, North Yorkshire, YO17 7AJ

01653 639 096
www.talbotmalton.co.uk

In the historic market town of Malton, the newly restored Talbot Hotel sits at the gateway to the Yorkshire Wolds, Moors and Coast and is just a short drive from the ancient city of York. As Malton is carving out a reputation as 'Yorkshire's Food Capital', when I heard that £4m was being spent on this lovely old building I sensed that something very exciting was on the cards; made even more so when James Martin agreed to be executive chef. I applaud his ethos of using only the best local and seasonal produce, so when the position of head chef arose it was an opportunity I was keen to grasp. Since then it's been an exhilarating journey, working with some remarkable local suppliers whilst establishing an exceptional reputation for food.

I first moved to Yorkshire in 2008 after 12 years working up and down the country with some of the UK's brightest chefs. My passion for game, foraging and gardening fits in well at the Talbot, where we source all our ingredients locally. Grouse, rabbit, fish and wild, edible ingredients, which all feature on the menu, will have been caught or picked within the region.

The style is modern British cuisine, which includes a wide range of modern techniques and classical flavour pairing. My inspiration comes from the seasonal fruit, vegetable and herbs that are grown in the hotel's garden and surrounding area. We seek out local food producers and champion the finest as our food heroes on our regularly changing menus.

But it's not all about food, much as I'd like to think so. From here you can discover the best of Yorkshire - Castle Howard is on the doorstep; hidden gems are just around the corner. A perfect base for sightseeing and for relaxing, the hotel is stylish and comfortable in a classical way.

Bedrooms are sumptuous and well equipped; staff are professional yet unstuffy and the walled gardens and meadow alongside the riverbank are a delight. The Talbot is unhurried and unspoilt; somewhere to return to again and again and, of course, enjoy very good food.

Craig Atchinson, Head Chef

Relish Restaurant Rewards
See page 003 for details.

Food and good service are the focus. The flavour, freshness and purity of the produce we use from the local area all contribute to the quality of food on the plate. Marry this with a warm atmosphere, stylish comfort and unobtrusive service and it's no wonder it's so popular. And we're delighted to have been awarded Trip Advisor's Certificate of Excellence and two AA rosettes.

CURED ORGANIC SALMON, SQUID INK QUAVER, CUCUMBER KETCHUP, SPRING ONIONS & PICKLED GINGER

SERVES 4

Dry Riesling, Trimbach, Alsace, Vintage 2011 (France). Trimbach is a superb family-run producer that dates back to 1626. Their wines typically have very fine fruit and high acidity. They describe Riesling as the 'King of the wines of Alsace'. The acidity and the fruit are a great match with light food with spices or a little kick.

Ingredients

Cured Salmon

200g salmon fillet (skin on)
150g table salt
150g caster sugar
$1/2$ vanilla pod

Cucumber Ketchup

1 cucumber (remove seeds)
50ml white wine vinegar
10g caster sugar
Ultratex (tapioca starch)

Squid Ink Quaver

100g tapioca pearls
500ml water
1 sachet squid ink
pinch of salt
200ml vegetable oil

Pickled Ginger

50g ginger (finely shredded)
75ml white wine vinegar
75g caster sugar
175ml water

Garnish

mixed salad leaves
spring onions (sliced)

Method

For The Cured Salmon (Prepare the day before)

In a food processor, blend the salt, sugar and vanilla pod. Pour all of the mixture evenly over the salmon and allow to cure in the fridge for at least 24 hours. Wash the fish in cold water and pat dry. Slice very thinly and lay on a tray until needed.

For The Squid Ink Quaver

Rinse the tapioca under a cold water tap for five minutes to remove the excess starch. In a saucepan, add the tapioca and the water and simmer for 12 minutes - it's really important that you stir constantly otherwise the tapioca will stick to the pan and burn. Strain off the excess liquid using a sieve and put the cooked tapioca into a bowl. Season with salt and add the squid ink. Spread as thin as possible on a tray lined with parchment paper and place in a very low oven (75°C) for 12 hours, or until dry and crisp. Heat the vegetable oil in a saucepan to 210°C - it's really important the oil is exactly at this temperature. Break small pieces of the dried tapioca and place into the hot oil (take care with this as the oil will bubble aggressively). The dried tapioca will instantly puff up into a light quaver-like crisp. Place onto kitchen paper to drain any fat and store at room temperature until needed.

For The Cucumber Ketchup

Blend the cucumber with the sugar and vinegar then pass through a fine sieve. Transfer the cucumber liquid into a bowl and whisk in the Ultratex, a little at a time, until the liquid resembles a ketchup consistency. If you can't get hold of Ultratex just miss it out and use the un-thickened liquid as a dressing.

For The Pickled Ginger

Put the finely shredded ginger in a saucepan. Cover with cold water and bring to a boil. Strain off the water, then add more cold water and boil again. Repeat three more times. This process tames the harsh flavour that ginger has. Once the ginger has been boiled five times, put the vinegar, sugar and water into a separate pan. Bring to a boil and pour onto the ginger. Do this a few hours in advance and it will keep indefinitely in the fridge.

To Serve

Arrange the slices of salmon to create a base to build on. Dot the ketchup around - you can add as much as you like depending on your personal preference. Using some mixed salad leaves and sliced spring onions, build a little salad with the pickled ginger and finally top it off with pieces of the squid ink quaver.

RIGGWELTER BEER BRAISED BEEF CHEEK, WILD GARLIC & PEARL BARLEY RISOTTO, MALTED ONIONS, SALSIFY & STOUT SAUCE

SERVES 4

🍷 *A pint of Black Sheep Riggwelter beer, or*
Santa Tresa, Nero d'Avola, Vintage 2006 (Sicily, Italy)

Ingredients

Braised Cheek

4 beef cheeks (sinew removed)
500ml Riggwelter beer from Black Sheep Brewery
2 cloves garlic
1 bunch fresh thyme
1 bay leaf
2ltrs beef stock

Pearl Barley Risotto

200g pearl barley
1ltr chicken stock
200g wild garlic
100ml double cream
30g Parmesan (grated)
lemon juice (few drops of)
salt (to taste)

Malted Onions

2 small white onions
500ml Riggwelter beer

Salsify

4 sticks salsify (peeled and washed)
2 tbsp vegetable oil

Method

For The Braised Cheeks
Put the beef cheeks in a suitable container, cover with the beer and add the garlic, bay leaf and thyme. Leave for at least six hours to marinate. Strain off the cheeks but keep the liquid. Transfer the marinade liquid into a large pan and bring to a boil. In a frying pan, brown the beef cheeks off until well caramelised on both sides. Add the cheeks to the stock pan with the marinade and cover with beef stock. Bring to a boil and simmer for around four to six hours, or until the cheeks are very tender. Skim any scum/fat from the surface to keep the stock clean. Remove the cheeks from the stock and reduce rapidly until thick and gelatinous. Put the cheeks back into the pan with the reduced stock and glaze the cheeks with the sticky reduction. Keep warm until needed. Use the glaze for the stout sauce by adding a little more beer to thin it out.

For The Pearl Barley Risotto
Put the chicken stock in a large pan and bring to a boil. Add the barley and boil for 12 minutes. Remove the barley and put into a medium sized saucepan. Bring the double cream to a boil and add the wild garlic. Cook the garlic for one minute and blend in a food processor until smooth. Pour the garlic cream onto the barley and heat on a medium flame. Just before serving, add the Parmesan, lemon juice and salt to your taste. If you have any wild garlic left use as an additional garnish by simply sweating in a little foaming butter for 30 seconds.

For The Malted Onions
Put the beer in a saucepan. Add the whole onions (with skin) and simmer until the onions are tender. Once cool enough to handle remove the skin and cut the onion into quarters. Separate the layers of onions and finish by frying in a hot pan until golden.

For The Salsify
Put the peeled salsify into a vacuum pack bag with the oil. Seal in a vacuum pack machine on full power. Cook in a water bath at 83°C until tender. Finish by cutting in half and frying in hot oil until golden - you can use the same pan as the onions. If you don't have access to a vacuum pack machine and water bath, you can simply boil the salsify in salted water with the juice of half a lemon for 12 minutes and finish in the same way.

To Serve
Spoon some of the barley risotto in the centre of the plate. Place the glazed cheek on top of the risotto. Arrange the onions and salsify around the plate, then drizzle over the sauce. This dish will really impress your friends and family and it's very cheap to produce.

ENGLISH STRAWBERRIES, AGED BALSAMIC, GARDEN MINT, WILD STRAWBERRY SORBET, SZECHWAN PEPPER MERINGUE

SERVES 4

Jacques Boncoeur Brut Champagne (France)
You can't beat strawberries and Champagne!

Ingredients

Strawberries

200g strawberries (stalks removed)
20ml 12-year-old balsamic vinegar

Wild Strawberry Sorbet

1kg wild strawberry purée
5ml white wine vinegar
80g pro-sorbet*
(*Pro-sorbet can be ordered online www.sosa.cat)

Szechwan Pepper Meringue

100g fresh egg whites
175g caster sugar
30g icing sugar
ground Szechwan pepper (pinch of)

Mint Oil

120g fresh mint
50ml vegetable oil

Garnish

lemon balm leaves (to garnish)

Method

For The Strawberries

Drizzle the balsamic over the strawberries and allow to marinate for at least 20 minutes before serving.

For The Sorbet (Make in advance and freeze)

Combine the ingredients and freeze.

For The Szechwan Pepper Meringue

Over a *bain-marie*, cook the egg white and sugar until they reach 75°C. Whisk in a machine until cold. Fold in the icing sugar. Spread thinly on parchment paper and dust lightly with the pepper. Dry in a warm oven at 75°C until crisp.

For The Mint Oil

Boil the mint in water for 30 seconds. Remove and squeeze out the excess water using a sieve. Put the mint into a blender with the oil and blitz for at least three minutes. Pour the oil through a sieve lined with muslin to extract the clean oil, which should have an intense mint flavour.

To Serve

Brush some of the aged balsamic on to a plate and use this to guide the rest of the presentation. Arrange the strawberries along the balsamic, cut some in half and quarters too. Using a dessert spoon, *quenelle* the sorbet on to the plate. Break pieces of the meringue and arrange randomly. Drizzle with the mint oil and finish with a few leaves of lemon balm.

314
TRUFFLE
RESTAURANT

20 Grange Road, Darlington, County Durham, DL1 5NG

01325 483 787
www.trufflerestaurant.co.uk

Situated in Darlington's fashionable west end, Truffle opened its doors to critical acclaim in September 2012, providing informal fine dining in a relaxed and stylish atmosphere. With a real dedication to the highest quality seasonal ingredients, we're happy to make use of the region's excellent larder. The kitchen team produces both an à la carte menu and a separate lunch menu. This doubles up as an 'early bird' evening menu. With a mezzanine cocktail bar level for pre and post-dinner drinks and 36 seats downstairs, sumptuous décor and a commitment to quality on all levels, Truffle is an intimate affair.

There is a 150-bin wine list, a dedicated sommelier and a cheese board of around 18 cheeses served table-side, with most of the cheese coming from the UK or France. Since opening, there have been cheese and wine evenings, wine-maker's dinners and tasting menu evenings.

Relish Restaurant Rewards
See page 003 for details.

Truffle is a collaboration of proprietors, Matthew and Emma Robertson, and industry specialists, head chef Adam Hegarty and sommelier Luke Richardson.
After working together at the Baltic, they both moved to create Truffle. Head chef Adam Hegarty is well known in the region; Adam trained with Terry Laybourne at his Michelin starred 21 Queen Street and then furthered his skills at Claridges, before returning to the region to run kitchens at The Black Door, Bayes and Six at the Baltic. Now running a small team in this intimate restaurant, Adam's flair for putting together great plates of food is being well received by regulars and newcomers alike.

BALLOTINE OF SALMON

SERVES 10

🍷 *2011 Montlouis, Frantz Saumon, Loire Valley (France)*

Ingredients

Salmon

2 x 600g sides salmon
cayenne pepper
salt (pinch of)
1 leaf gelatine
1 bunch fresh dill (finely chopped)
1 bunch flat leaf parsley (finely chopped)

Fromage Blanc

10g shallot (finely chopped)
200g fromage blanc
1/2 clove garlic
30ml lemon juice
7g salt
6 drops tabasco
30ml double cream
mixed herbs
2 tbsp double cream

Garnish

150g fresh langoustines
24g chives
20g caviar
50g sorrel
vinaigrette

Method

For The Salmon (Prepare the day before)

Cure the salmon with the cayenne pepper and salt for 45 minutes, rinse then pat dry. Place one side of the salmon, skin side down, on a piece of clingfilm. Cut the gelatine into equal strips and place them along the fillet. Top with the second side of salmon (skin side up). Roll the entire salmon in the chopped herbs, wrap tightly and tie both ends to create a cylinder. Place in clean muslin and tie in equally spaced intervals with ten pieces of string. Poach in shallow water, just covering the salmon, for five minutes per kilogram (so seven minutes in total). Turn the salmon half way through. Remove from the heat and allow to rest for a further seven minutes. Add ice to the water to cool it rapidly. Remove and refrigerate overnight.

Chef's Tip

When chopping the herbs, let them air dry for ten minutes before coating your salmon. This gives a more even coat.

For The Fromage Blanc

Sweat off shallots in a little olive oil until soft but not coloured. Allow to cool. Mix the cheese with the shallot, garlic, lemon juice, salt and tabasco. Fold in the double cream a little at a time, then add the herbs. Leave to rest.

To Serve

Slice the salmon into 2.5cm slices and place one in the centre of the plate. Surround with four to five *quenelles* of fromage blanc, topped with chives and sorrel. Alternate with pieces of langoustine brushed with vinaigrette and topped with caviar.

VEAL BLANQUETTE WITH CRAYFISH & TARRAGON

SERVES 8

🍷 *2011 Minervois Blanc, 'L'Inattendu',
Clos du Gravillas, Languedoc (France)*

Ingredients

Veal

2 veal tenderloins
salt (pinch of)
250g flour
4 tbsp canola oil
500ml veal stock (reduced to a 150ml glaze)

Garnish

250g fava beans (shelled)
250g peas
24 baby carrots (orange, yellow and red)
16 pearl onions
16 asparagus tips

Sauce

32 crayfish
1 tbsp butter
24 morel stalks
1 tbsp shallot (diced)
500ml veal stock
500ml shellfish stock
25ml cream
2 sprigs tarragon
2 tbsp lemon juice
salt (pinch of)

To Finish

100g butter
24 morel tops
crayfish tails

250ml chicken stock

Method

For The Veal

Cut the loin into 2.5cm cubes. Season with salt, dredge in flour and pat off any excess. Heat some oil in a saucepan and sear the loin over a high heat to medium rare (one minute on each side). Ensure the loin is evenly brown, then remove from the heat. Drain and discard any excess oil. Add the veal stock to the pan and baste until medium. Rest in a warm place for ten minutes.

> **Chef's Tip**
>
> We use a wonderful British veal loin, but pork loin would make a fine substitute.

For The Garnish

Blanch the vegetables in salted water.

For The Sauce

Bring a pot of salted water to a boil. Add the crayfish and cook for two minutes. Transfer to a bowl of ice water. Once cooked, peel and keep the tails for the final assembly.

Melt the butter in a large pan over a medium heat. Add the crayfish and stir, while crushing with a wooden spoon. Add the morel stalks, shallots and sweat down until soft. Add the lobster stock and reduce by half. Add the veal stock and reduce by half again. Bring to a simmer then add the cream, tarragon and lemon zest. Remove from the heat and cover. Steep for 20 minutes, then strain. Season with lemon juice and salt.

To Serve

Melt the butter in a large pan on medium heat. Add the morels and cook for one minute. Add the *blanched* vegetables, crayfish tails and the chicken stock. Toss lightly to glaze. Place the veal cubes onto the plate and four crayfish tails around the veal. Blend the sauce with a hand blender and drizzle around the dish, being careful not to cover the vegetables.

CHOCOLATE & PASSION FRUIT

SERVES 8

Jurançon, Magendia de Lapeyre Pyrenees
(France)

Ingredients

Chocolate Cylinders

350g dark chocolate (broken up)
acetate (to form cylinder)

Chocolate Cream

250ml double cream
500ml whole milk
360g dark chocolate
12 tbsp caster sugar
6 egg yolks

Passion Fruit Foam

450g passion fruit purée
3 leaves gelatine
icing sugar (to taste)

Banana Ice Cream

250g ripe banana
400g natural yoghurt
100ml double cream
80g sugar

Garnish

biscuit crumbs

Method

For The Chocolate Cylinders

Temper the chocolate. For this you will need a digital probe thermometer. Set aside 55g of the chocolate. Place the rest in a glass mixing bowl and put on the heat until the chocolate has melted. Give the chocolate a stir until the core temperature is 45°C - no more than two degrees higher than this. To make the cylinders, cut out a rectangle of acetate and stick around a rolling pin using some tape. Pour the melted chocolate around the rolling pin, so that the acetate is completely covered. Place in the fridge to set for an hour or so.

For The Banana Ice Cream

Peel and slice the bananas. Blend the bananas with the yoghurt, double cream and sugar. Churn in an ice cream maker or freeze for 22 hours.

For The Chocolate Cream

Boil the cream and milk together. Whisk in the egg yolks and sugar until well combined. Once the mix is up to 81°C, put the chocolate in, stir until melted, then remove from the heat. Set in the fridge for eight hours.

For The Passion Fruit Foam

Put 400g of the passion fruit purée in a bowl. Soften the gelatine in the remaining purée. Warm the gelatine and purée mixture and mix together. Add to the rest of the purée then add icing sugar to taste.

To Serve

Brush some of the chocolate cream across the plate. Set the cylinder upon this wipe on one side of the plate. Half fill the cylinder with the chocolate cream and top up with the passionfruit foam. On the other side of the wipe, sprinkle some biscuit crumbs. Finally, set a scoop of the banana yoghurt ice cream on top.

> **Chef's Tip**
> A digital temperature probe is vital for this and is a sound investment!

324
THE WENSLEYDALE HEIFER

Main Street, West Witton, Yorkshire, DL8 4LS

01969 622 322
www.wensleydaleheifer.co.uk

The Wensleydale Heifer is situated in the idyllic village of West Witton in the heart of the Yorkshire Dales. Between Leyburn and Hawes, it is one of the most beautiful areas of the country.

The Wensleydale Heifer's award-winning dining and accommodation has attracted guests from near and far. Renowned for its quirkiness and charm, the AA five star restaurant with rooms is a joint venture between father and son, Lewis and David Moss.

Creating the Heifer's stunning dishes, that have delighted and impressed critics and customers alike, is a dedicated team of five chefs, led by John Barley, who have trained in several different countries. Their philosophy in the kitchen is 'keep it simple' - source the best quality ingredients, cook them well and let the natural flavours speak for themselves.

Diners can enjoy the finest fish and seafood that the British Isles has to offer and fresh local produce, which makes each dish on the Heifer's signature menu, à la carte menu and table d'hôte menu that little bit more special.

Our restaurant is contemporary decadence, with its chocolate leather chairs, linen table cloths and Doug Hyde artwork; great for an evening out or celebrating a special occasion. The Fish Bar - with sea grass flooring, wooden tables and rattan chairs - is perfect for a less formal dining experience. Guests can also enjoy the fine weather in our restaurant garden.

If guests need a rest after over-indulging or simply want a relaxing weekend away or a short holiday, The Wensleydale Heifer has 13 luxurious rooms, each with its own unique theme and all the charm of a 17th Century inn. Whether a whisky, Champagne or chocolate devotee; a movie, racing, real ale or animal lover, guests are sure to find a room to suit them down to the ground.

Our lounge is the perfect spot to relax with a morning coffee, read the newspapers, relax with a pre-dinner aperitif or enjoy one of our handpicked malt whiskies. With a roaring log fire and soft leather furnishings, it's sometimes difficult to motivate guests to leave and enjoy the stunning scenery.

Relish Restaurant Rewards
See page 003 for details.

Their philosophy in the kitchen is 'keep it simple' - source the best quality ingredients, cook them well and let the natural flavours speak for themselves.

WHITBY CRAB TIAN, DUO OF SALMON GRAVADLAX, BLUSH TOMATO, WILD GARLIC & ASPARAGUS DRESSING

SERVES 4

 Picpoul de Pinet
(France)

A refreshing mineral mouth feel with a zippy appley bite and a bone dry long finish. Perfect with seafood.

Ingredients

Salmon

400g salmon (divided into 2 pieces vertically)
1 vanilla pod
170g Maldon salt
150g sugar
5g parsley (chopped)
5g dill (chopped)
5g coriander (chopped)
1 lemon (juice of)
1 tbsp Dijon mustard

Potato Mayonnaise

230g new potatoes
1 red onion (diced)
1 lemon (juice of)
2 tbsp good full fat mayonnaise
5g dill (chopped)

Crab

125g white crabmeat (picked)
2 sprigs dill
small bunch chives
salt and pepper

Dressing

6 spears extra thick asparagus (cooked)
12 sunblush tomatoes (half chopped, half diced)
1 lemon (juice of)
1 lime (juice of)
4 sprigs wild garlic
70ml extra virgin olive oil

Garnish

red amaranth
micro rocket

Method

For The Salmon And Gravadlax (Prepare one day before)

Blend the vanilla, 85g of salt and 75g of sugar into a fine powder and cover one half of the salmon with it.

Leave for one day and then wash. Top with half of the chopped dill and the Dijon mustard and thinly slice.

Blend the rest of the salt, the rest of the sugar, the lemon juice and the rest of the chopped herbs. Cover the other half of the salmon with the mixture and leave for one day. Wash, then chop into 2.5cm squares.

For The Potato Mayonnaise Base

Boil the new potatoes for 20 minutes or until soft. Allow to cool, then dice. Add the onion, lemon juice, dill, mayonnaise and mix.

For The Crab

Mix the ingredients together.

For The Dressing (Prepare the day before)

Slow roast the sunblush tomatoes with a drizzle of olive oil overnight at 65°C.

Thinly slice the asparagus diagonally and then mix gently into the tomatoes and other ingredients.

To Serve

Warm a pan with a little olive oil.

Place a cutter on the centre of the plate. Add the potato mayonnaise base, then top with the thinly sliced gravadlax. For the next layer, add the crab. Remove the cutter.

Sear the salmon chunks over a medium heat and then place on top of the crab. Finally, drizzle the dressing around the tian.

TRIO OF LOBSTER - LOBSTER THERMIDOR TAIL, LOBSTER & PRAWN PIE, CRISPY LOBSTER CLAW WITH A TOMATO & BROWN SHRIMP SALSA

SERVES 4

🍷 *Gavi*
(Italy)

Ingredients

2 x 700g lobsters

Lobster Tails

85g Gruyère or Comté cheese
2 x large king scallops
12.5g Panko (Japanese breadcrumbs)

Fish Cream Sauce

1 fennel bulb
1 clove garlic, 1 stick celery, 1 onion
200ml white wine
200ml fish stock
35ml brandy
2 star anise
400ml double cream

Thermidor Sauce

$2/3$ fish cream sauce (prepared from above)
10g English mustard

Lobster And Prawn Pie

70g Greenland prawns
35g capers
2 Maris Piper potatoes (peeled, chopped and
mashed with 25g unsalted butter)

Crispy Claws

1 egg (beaten)
1 tbsp plain flour
12.5g Panko (Japanese breadcrumbs)

Salsa

35g brown shrimp
6 blush tomatoes (finely chopped)
1 red onion (finely chopped)
5g coriander, 10g dill, 5g tarragon, 10g basil
(finely chopped)
fresh lemon juice (squeeze of)

Method

Preheat fryer to 180°C. Preheat oven to 200°C.

To Prepare The Lobster
Stab lobsters through the back of the head and then add to boiling water for eight minutes. Remove and run under cold water until cold. Cut each lobster in half, directly through the back of the lobster, discarding the brain and the tract pipe. Crack the claws and arms and remove the meat - keep the claws whole. Remove the tails with the meat inside the shell. Once completed on all the lobster halves, flip the tails over so the red tail meat is showing.

For The Fish Cream Sauce
Peel and slice the onion, fennel bulb, garlic and celery. Cook for five minutes on a low heat, stirring occasionally so as not to colour too much. Add the wine, fish stock, brandy and star anise, reduce by half and then add the double cream. Bring to a boil, season well, then drain. Divide the sauce into two pans, one third in one (fish cream) and two thirds in the other (for the thermidor sauce).

For Thermidor Sauce
Add the mustard to the pan with two thirds of the fish cream sauce and bring to a boil. Set aside.

For The Lobster Tails
Chop the scallops into quarters. Remove the meat from the lobster tail shell and chop into three nuggets. Place the meat back into the shell, alternating with the scallop quarters. Add the cheese onto the lobster tails. Pour over the thermidor sauce and top with the Panko breadcrumbs and set aside until needed.

For The Lobster And Prawn Pie
Use a small pie dish, approximately 5cm x 5cm. Put the capers, prawns and two nuggets of the arm meat from the lobster in the pie dish. Add a few drops of the fish cream sauce (see above) and top with the mash. Place into a preheated oven for four minutes, then place the tails in the oven too and cook for a further six minutes.

For The Crispy Claws
Flour the claws, shells removed, then coat in the beaten egg and then the Panko breadcrumbs. When the pie comes out of the oven, pop the claw into the fryer and cook for three minutes.

For The Salsa
Mix all the ingredients together.

To Serve
Plate as pictured. Serve with the left over thermidor sauce.

STRAWBERRY PANNA COTTA

SERVES 4

🍷 *Whispering Angel*
(France)

Ingredients

Strawberry Jelly

150ml Boiron strawberry purée
$^1/_2$ lemon (juice of)
1 leaf basil
1 leaf gelatine (softened in cold water)

Panna Cotta

300ml double cream, 75ml whole milk
150g caster sugar
3 star anise
$1^1/_2$ gold leaves gelatine (softened in cold water)

Strawberry Glass

100g strawberry purée
25g Isomalt

Strawberry Sorbet

350g strawberries
75g caster sugar
$1^1/_2$ lemons (juice of)

Short Crumb Base

50g plain flour, 85g rice flour
25g caster sugar
50g butter
5g salt

Poppy Seed Pebbles

75g egg white
55g caster sugar
1 lime (juice of)
5g almonds, 10g poppy seeds

Strawberry Black Pepper Marinade

150g strawberry purée
150g raspberry purée
12 black peppercorns
50ml balsamic vinegar
1 lime (juice of)
3 whole strawberries

Garnish

basil leaves

4 x 100ml moulds

Method

For The Strawberry Jelly

In a pan, bring the purée, lemon juice and basil to a boil. Add the gelatine, dissolve, then sieve. Pour $^1/_2$cm depth of the sieved mixture into each panna cotta mould and set in the fridge.

For The Panna Cotta (Prepare the day before)

Place the cream, milk, sugar and star anise in a heavy bottomed saucepan on a medium heat. Bring to a boil, then remove from the heat and set aside for one hour to infuse.

Sieve, then return to the pan and bring back to a boil. Stir in the gelatine and set aside. When the jelly is set and the panna cotta mix is lukewarm, pour onto the jelly and return to the fridge to set, preferably overnight.

For The Strawberry Glass (Prepare the day before)

Bring the purée to a boil, add the Isomalt and boil for five minutes.

Spread thinly onto a silicone mat (so you can see through it) and bake overnight in the oven at 55°C. When it's ready it will be translucent and crisp. Break into shards and store in an airtight container.

For The Strawberry Sorbet (Prepare in advance and freeze)

Blend the strawberries with the sugar and lemon, then bring to a boil in a pan. Leave to cool then add to an ice cream machine and churn.

For The Pebbles

Whip the egg whites into soft peaks. Add the caster sugar until a firm meringue is achieved. Add the lime juice. Divide the egg white mixture into two, add the almonds and poppy seeds into one half and then fold in the other half. Place into a piping bag and pipe little drops (of 2 to 3cm circumference) onto a silicone mat.

Put in the oven at 110°C for 90 minutes until dried out. Store in an airtight container.

For The The Short Crumb Base

Place all the ingredients into a food processor and blend until fine crumbs are achieved. Bake for eight minutes at 190°C until golden brown. Set aside to cool and place in an airtight container until needed.

For The Marinade

Boil the purées, peppercorns, vinegar and lime juice. Sieve, blend, cool. Dice the strawberries and drop them into the marinade. Leave for one hour.

To Serve

Run the moulds under the hot water tap for a few seconds to release the panna cottas. Assemble as in picture.

334
WENTBRIDGE HOUSE

Wentbridge House Hotel, The Great North Road, Wentbridge, Pontefract, West Yorkshire, WF8 3JJ

01977 620 444
www.wentbridgehouse.co.uk

Wentbridge House is a beautiful Georgian country house hotel. The building dates from 1700 and we have been open as a hotel since 1960. The hotel is set in 20 acres of gardens and grounds in the village of Wentbridge, West Yorkshire. Steeped in history and surrounded by century-old trees, Wentbridge is a hidden gem and offers a luxurious and peaceful retreat from everyday life.

The hotel is independently owned and run with a great deal of care and dedication, ensuring the warm welcome, excellent service and restful atmosphere you would expect of a country house hotel.

Wentbridge House has always been passionate about food. Executive chef Scott Hessel places great emphasis on using fresh, locally sourced produce and the best of British ingredients to produce a wide range of both classic and contemporary dishes.

Experienced and creative chefs offer two dining options. The Fleur de Lys Restaurant is a true fine-dining experience and holds two AA Rosettes. Local, seasonal produce and the best of British ingredients are combined to create innovative and delicious dishes alongside one of the best and most extensive wine lists in Yorkshire, which features old favourites and a few surprises.

The hugely popular Wentbridge Brasserie is slightly more contemporary and offers an alternative for those wanting simple, tasty comfort food in elegant surroundings for lunch and dinner, seven days a week.

 Relish Restaurant Rewards
See page 003 for details.

A warm welcome awaits at Wentbridge House - a perfect venue for private dining and entertaining, whether on a grand or intimate scale. Hotel manager, Catherine Harrild, and her team, focus on delivering excellent food, service and hospitality in a relaxed atmosphere which appeals both to hotel guests and the local community.

MACKEREL 'ASIAN FLAVOURS'

SERVES 4

🍷 *Riesling Réserve 2010, F.E. Trimbach, Alsace (France)*

Ingredients

Miso Grilled Mackerel

2 mackerel fillets
100ml Sake
100ml mirin
500g miso paste
250g caster sugar

Cucumber Kimchi

1/2 cucumber
1 tbsp rice wine vinegar
1 chilli (finely diced)
chilli powder (good pinch of)
1 tbsp honey

Smoked Mackerel Spring Roll

2 smoked mackerel fillets (flaked)
2 tsp oyster sauce
1/2 carrot (*julienne*)
1/4 Chinese cabbage (*julienne*)
50g beansprouts
spring roll pastry (packet of)

Mackerel Tartare

2 mackerel fillets
1 tsp salt
1 tsp sugar
1 tsp yuzu
2 tsp soy sauce

Wasabi Mayonnaise

wasabi
mayonnaise

Garnish

wasabi
mayonnaise
mango purée
peanuts (roasted)
small bunch chives
rice stick noodles
caviar of choice
black sesame seeds
micro herbs

Method

For The Miso Mackerel

Trim the mackerel fillets and check for any bones. For the miso marinade, combine the Sake, mirin, sugar and miso.
In a bowl, mix until all the sugar is dissolved, then brush onto the fillets and leave to marinate for four hours.

For The Cucumber Kimchi

Peel and slice the cucumber in half lengthways, then thinly slice. In a small container, mix the finely diced chilli, chilli powder, honey and vinegar. Put the sliced cucumber in with the chilli and vinegar mix. Leave to marinate for a couple of hours, or longer in a sealed jar.

For The Spring Rolls

Sauté the carrot, cabbage and beansprouts and season with oyster sauce. Reserve and cool. Mix in the flaked smoked mackerel. Assemble by wrapping two teaspoons of the mixture in the spring roll pastry, then cover with a dry cloth and refrigerate until needed.

For The Mackerel Tartare

Sprinkle the fillets with about a teaspoon of salt and a teaspoon of sugar and leave to marinate for 15 minutes. Wash off the salt and sugar and dice the mackerel into even sized pieces.
Make the dressing for the tartare, but don't mix through until the last minute before serving. For the dressing, mix one teaspoon of yuzu with the two teaspoons of soy sauce.

For The Rice Sticks

Heat a 2cm of oil in pan, get it really hot ,but be mindful of it catching fire. Add a single rice stick at a time until it puffs up. Drain on some kitchen paper.

For The Wasabi Mayonnaise

Mix a little wasabi through the mayonnaise until you get the taste of wasabi, but be careful not to get too much heat.

To Serve

Grill the miso mackerel and deep fry the spring rolls. This will take about three minutes. To season and assemble the mackerel tartare, mix through the yuzu and soy dressing until you can just taste it over the fish. Place a small neat pile of the tartare on the plate and garnish with chives, black sesame seeds and caviar. Next make a small pile of the drained cucumber kimchi, this is to place the grilled mackerel on. Cut the ends off the spring rolls and cut diagonally in half. Stand the two ends up on the plate. Decorate the plate with small squeezy blobs of wasabi mayonnaise, mango purée, roast peanuts, micro herbs and crispy noodles.

LAMB WELLINGTON 'MEDITERRANEAN FLAVOURS'

SERVES 4

🍷 *Rioja Reserva 2007, Vina Izadi, Rioja Alavesa (Spain)*

Ingredients

Lamb Wellington

4 x 180g lamb loin eye pieces
500g butter puff pastry
4 pancakes
50g Kalamata olives (finely chopped)
1 tbsp tarragon (chopped)
100g chicken breast
1 egg
150ml cream
4 tsp cream and 2 egg yolks (to glaze)

Garnish

4 baby fennel
1 punnet cherry tomatoes
fresh thyme
50g Kalamata olives (halved and stone removed)
100g feta cheese (cubed)
2 courgettes

Mint And Basil Oil

large bunch basil and mint
200ml vegetable oil
200ml olive oil

Method

For The Wellington

First you need to seal the lamb fillets on all sides in a very hot pan with a little oil and seasoning. You are just looking to seal the lamb and not cook it. Reserve and cool. Next you need to make the chicken farce or mousse which binds the whole wellington together. In a food processor, blend the chicken breast and purée till smooth. Season, add the egg and re-purée. At this point you may need to scrape down the mix with a spatula. Next, add the cream and blend quickly so as not to split the cream. Add the finely chopped olives and tarragon. Reserve and chill for two hours.

To assemble the wellingtons, cut out a piece of puff pastry 14cm x 18cm. Cover with a trimmed pancake, spread on a thin layer of mousse and place of the lamb in the centre. Roll the wellington and squeeze the edges together to seal it all up - you can, at this stage, brush with egg wash. I use two egg yolks and four teaspoons of cream mixed together to give that brilliant shine when cooked.

For The Garnish

Cut the cherry tomatoes in half, season and sprinkle with thyme. Leave in a very low oven until they have half dried. Cook the baby fennel for seven to eight minutes until it's just soft to the point of a knife. Slice the courgettes lengthways, really thin, and marinate with olive oil and salt.

For The Mint And Basil Oil

Blanch the herbs in boiling water for ten seconds and refresh in cold water. Place the drained and dried herbs in a blender with the oil and blitz for one to two minutes. After blitzing the herbs, pass through a fine tea towel or muslin and leave to drain for an hour or so - this will result in bright green and clear oil.

To Serve

Cook the lamb for 16 minutes in a preheated oven at 180°C and rest for two minutes. Arrange all the garnishes on the plate, making sure you warm the baby fennel ahead of time. Carve the ends of the wellington and then cut in half to sit it proudly on the serving plate.

PISTACHIO PANNA COTTA & SUMMER FRUITS

SERVES 4

🍷 *Sticky Mickey Late Harvest Sauvignon Blanc 2009, Eradus (New Zealand)*

Ingredients

Panna Cotta
300ml milk
200ml cream
1 tbsp pistachio paste
40g caster sugar
2 leaves gelatine

Macaroons
Step 1
185g icing sugar
185g ground almonds
2 medium egg whites

Step 2
2 medium egg whites
2 drops lemon juice
185g sugar
3 tbsp water

Garnish
mixed fresh berries (of choice)
strawberry sorbet
mini meringues

Method

For The Panna Cotta

Warm the milk, cream and pistachio paste. Soak the gelatine in cold water. Add the sugar and gelatine to the milk and cream. Mix well and strain. Divide the mix equally between four moulds and chill for at least four hours.

For The Macaroons

Heat the oven to 170°C.

Step 1
Combine all the ingredients in a large bowl and mix thoroughly. This is the time to add any flavourings that you may have, if you so desire.

Step 2
Crack the egg whites into a bowl and add the lemon juice - have a whisk ready at hand. Put the sugar and water in a pan along with any colouring you may have, bring to a boil. Use a sugar thermometer to measure when the mixture gets to 112°C. At this point, start whisking the egg whites until they form stiff peaks. When the sugar reaches a temperature of 118°C, take off the heat and add slowly to the egg whites whilst still whisking. Make sure that the sugar is poured in slowly and doesn't touch the side of the bowl or the whisk, so as not to lose any of the sugar mix.

Now add the meringue (from step 2) to step 1 in three batches. Don't be too worried about knocking the air out as you want the final mix to be shiny. Pipe into even round shapes on baking parchment lined trays and leave to dry and form a crust. Bake the macaroons for eight minutes, remove from the oven and leave to cool completely. You can sandwich the macaroons together with jam or a little butter cream.

To Serve

Turn out the panna cotta, garnish with the little meringues, a *roche* of sorbet and a mix of fresh berries. Serve with your homemade macaroons.

344
THE WESTWOOD RESTAURANT

New Walk, Beverley, East Yorkshire, HU17 7AE

01482 881 999
www.thewestwood.co.uk

The Westwood offers modern British food in relaxed, informal surroundings. Located in the grounds of Beverley's Georgian, Grade II listed, former court house, its modern, comfortable interior complements perfectly the classic features and charm of this historic building. When the sun is out, there's no better place for a meal than out on the terrace.

Our aim is this - great food, a warm welcome and a polished service to match. We also believe in making the most of the seasons so our menu is constantly changing to bring you the best of locally sourced produce. The Westwood experience is certainly one you'll enjoy, whether for a light lunch, meeting family and friends or a special occasion.

Twins Matthew and Michele Barker, are the partnership and passion behind The Westwood. The Westwood has focused on casual dining and delivered the highest of standards since opening in 2007, making it one of East Yorkshire's favourite places to enjoy food.

Matthew and Michele's career paths and individual journeys prior to opening the Westwood has taken them around the world. Their influences come from as far away as Sydney, London and New York, and their mentors include Sir Richard Branson, Jean-George Vongerichten and Alain Ducasse to name a few - some of the best in the hospitality business.

Relish Restaurant Rewards
See page 003 for details.

With the long term vision of a 'local' quality restaurant, Matthew, Michele and their team use high quality, locally sourced ingredients to serve up the best the region has to offer in innovative and classical ways.

BRIDLINGTON CRAB ON 'TOAST', SWEET PICKLED CUCUMBER, WATERCRESS, DILL CREME FRAICHE

SERVES 4

Conde Villar Alvarinho, 2011
(Portugul)

Abundant, yet elegant floral scents paired with pleasant and fresh fragrances of lemon and orange tree blossom.

Ingredients

4 large crabs (picked white crab and picked brown meat, separated)
1 loaf sourdough bread

Dill Crème Fraîche

3 tbsp crème fraîche
1 tbsp mayonnaise
20g fresh dill (chopped)
1/2 lemon (juice)
salt and pepper

Sweet Pickled Cucumber

1 cucumber
50g fresh dill (chopped)
5 tbsp white wine vinegar
1 tbsp caster sugar

Brown Crabmeat

brown crabmeat
2 tbsp tomato ketchup
1/2 tbsp English mustard
Lea and Perrins (splash)
Tabasco sauce (splash)
50g butter (*clarified*)
salt and pepper (to taste)

Garnish

English asparagus (*blanched* and chilled)
micro baby watercress
crab claws

Method

For The Dill Crème Fraîche

Combine the crème fraîche, mayonnaise, lemon juice and chopped dill. Season with salt and pepper. Set aside in the refrigerator until needed.

For The Sweet Pickled Cucumber

Combine the vinegar and sugar, then whisk until sugar is dissolved. Finish with chopped dill. Halve the cucumber lengthways. Using a teaspoon, channel out the centre of the cucumber, then slice and add to the pickling liquor. Pickle the cucumber for at least three hours in the refrigerator.

For The Brown Crabmeat

Place the brown crabmeat only in a food processor with the tomato ketchup, English mustard, Lea and Perrins, Tabasco and salt and pepper. Blend until smooth. At that stage, *clarify* the butter in the microwave until melted and slowly pour into the food processor to finish. Pass the mixture through a sieve to eliminate any shell. Chill and set aside for an hour.

> **Chef's Tip**
>
> If you find picking your own fresh crabmeat daunting, most good fish merchants will sell pre-picked fresh white and brown crabmeat.

To Serve

Toast four slices of sourdough with olive oil, arrange on four plates. Place the white crabmeat on top then, using a hot dessert spoon, *quenelle* the brown crabmeat and dill crème fraîche onto the plate. Finish with pickled cucumber, micro baby watercress, pre-*blanched* asparagus and a crab claw.

FOUR HOUR COOKED PORCHETTA, JERUSALEM ARTICHOKE PUREE & SWEET & SOUR BABY CARROTS, AMPLEFORTH ABBEY CIDER & ROSEMARY JUS

SERVES 10 - 12

Charles Smith, "Kung Fu girl" Riesling, Washington State, 2011 (USA)

Aromatic, smooth, vibrant and tasty, bursting with delicious stone fruit and citrus notes.

Ingredients

Pork Belly

1 whole pork belly (bone off, rind off)
5 ltrs vegetable oil
$1/2$ bulb garlic
50g sage (chopped)
50g rosemary (chopped)
3 lemons (zest)
2 tbsp fennel seeds (toasted)
2 tbsp honey
salt and pepper

Sweet And Sour Carrots

6 bunches baby carrots
1 ltr white wine vinegar
500g caster sugar
1 sprig thyme
1 sprig rosemary
1 clove garlic

Jerusalem Artichoke Purée

1kg Jerusalem artichokes (peeled)
200ml double cream
100ml chicken stock
salt
white pepper
1 sprig thyme
2 lemons (juice of for lemon water)

Ampleforth Cider And Rosemary Jus

500ml Ampleforth Abbey Cider
100g shallots (sliced)
1 sprig rosemary
250ml veal stock
250ml chicken stock

Method

For The Porchetta

Season the meat side with salt and pepper, drizzle with honey and top generously with sage, rosemary, garlic, lemon zest and fennel seeds. Roll tightly lengthways and tie with butcher's string at intervals of one inch to produce a long cannon. Using a deep roasting tray, submerge the belly in the vegetable oil with half a bulb of garlic and a sprig of rosemary. Cook for four hours at 120°C. After cooking, leave to cool in the vegetable oil. Portion into 5cm discs when chilled.

> **Chef's Tip**
> Make the porchetta the day before so it has time to cool in the liquid and chill overnight.

For The Sweet And Sour Carrots

Gently clean the carrots with a scourer. Combine the white wine vinegar and sugar and bring to a boil. Add the clove of garlic, thyme, rosemary and carrots. Simmer until the carrots are just cooked, with a slightly nutty texture. Remove from the heat and cool in the liquid.

For The Jerusalem Artichoke Purée

Slice the artichokes into lemon water. Using a heavy bottomed pan, heat the cream, chicken stock and thyme. Drain the artichokes and simmer in the cream and stock until tender. Season with salt and white pepper, blend, then pass through a fine sieve to finish.

For The Ampleforth Abbey Cider And Rosemary Jus

Place the Ampleforth Abbey Cider, shallots and rosemary in a saucepan. Reduce by two thirds and add the veal and chicken stock. Reduce again by two thirds, then pass the jus through a sieve and check the seasoning.

To Serve

Roast the porchetta in the oven at 180°C for 12 to 15 minutes until golden. Meanwhile, warm through the artichoke purée and sweet and sour carrots. Arrange as pictured and finish with Ampleforth Cider and rosemary jus.

WARM PEANUT BUTTER CHOCOLATE FONDANT, PEANUT BUTTER ICE CREAM & PEANUT BRITTLE

SERVES 6

Maury Grenat Els, Pyreneus 2009 (France)
Deliciously sweet red wine, full bodied and rich with intense flavours and aromas of dried red fruit, chocolate and coffee.

Ingredients

Chocolate Fondant

125g unsalted butter
125g dark chocolate (60 - 70% cocoa)
2 whole eggs
2 egg yolks
4 tbsp caster sugar
2 tbsp plain flour (sieved)

Peanut Butter Filling

150g milk chocolate (30 - 40% cocoa, broken into pieces)
25g unsalted butter
75ml double cream
20g caster sugar
2 tbsp coarse peanut butter
1 whole free range egg
1 free range egg yolk

Peanut Brittle

100g caster sugar
50ml glucose syrup
1/4 tsp salt
25ml water
130g unsalted peanuts (*blanched*)
2 tbsp unsalted butter (softened)
1 tsp baking soda

Garnish

peanut butter or vanilla ice cream
icing sugar (for dusting)

Method

For The Dark Chocolate Fondant Mixture

Melt chocolate and butter together in a heat-proof bowl over a saucepan of simmering water. Meanwhile, in a separate bowl, whisk the whole eggs, yolks and sugar until it's a pale, creamy colour. Carefully fold the melted warm chocolate mixture into the whisked eggs. Fold in the sieved flour.

For The Peanut Butter Filling

Heat the cream, butter and sugar to boiling point. Add the broken up milk chocolate, the coarse peanut butter, eggs and egg yolks. Stir until all ingredients are blended together. Place in the fridge and chill overnight.

> **Chef's Tip**
> Make the peanut butter filling the day before.

For The Peanut Brittle

Grease a large baking sheet and set aside. In a large, heavy bottomed saucepan, bring the sugar, glucose syrup, salt and water to a boil over a medium heat. Stir until the sugar is dissolved. Stir in the peanuts. Cook until golden caramel in colour and the peanuts are toasted. Remove from the heat. Immediately stir in the butter, then the baking soda. (Note: this will double in size!) Pour very carefully onto the greased baking sheet as the mixture is very hot. Using a fork, spread evenly over the baking sheet. Leave to cool. Snap the brittle into pieces. The brittle keeps well in an airtight container for two weeks.

To Serve

Spoon the chocolate fondant mix into six ramekins, 8cm diameter x 5cm deep, until half full, then place a teaspoon of milk chocolate peanut butter filling in the centre. Spoon over some of the chocolate fondant mixture to finish. Place in a preheated oven at 180°C for ten minutes. When cooked, serve with crushed brittle on top, peanut butter ice cream and dust with icing sugar.

355
FOOD FIT FOR A DUKE

Being based in the North East, Relish Publications were delighted to play a part in the region's culinary scene by sponsoring The North East Culinary and Trade Association Chef of the Year.

The Salon Culinaire at Newcastle Civic Centre is a two day festival of the region's cooking skills and culinary talent. It features colleges and professionals from across the North East, competing to demonstrate the significant and diverse range of skills needed to work in a professional kitchen. NECTA is an established part of culinary life in the North East, for industry professionals and emerging new talent.

Relish wanted to work alongside NECTA and recognise the contribution this body makes to the development of our fine dining sector. Many of the chefs featured in our existing books have started their careers in these Further Education colleges, learning the essential skills which are required by all professional chefs.

After a Masterchef-style competition, Gabor Pustzai, head chef at The Duke of Wellington in Newton, Northumberland won the prestigious Chef of the Year award. This is a fantastic achievement for a talented chef from our region and demonstrates the culinary flair being brought through in the North East's many fine-dining establishments.

Gabor, who is originally from Keszthely in the south of Hungary, started out at the George Hotel in Jesmond and has worked in many Michelin starred kitchens including the world number one ranked restaurant, Noma, in Copenhagen.

To find out more about Gabor, and to sample some of his mouthwatering recipes, turn to page 142 or visit The Duke of Wellington in Newton, Northumberland.

356
RELISH NORTH EAST & YORKSHIRE LARDER

THE DELI AROUND THE CORNER
61 Hotspur Street, Tynemouth, NE30 4EE
T: 0191 259 0086
www.thedeliaroundthecorner.co.uk

This successful deli has a selection of over 50 cheeses and traditional deli products. They also create fantastic bespoke wedding cakes, gourmet hampers and gifts and they also offer solutions for outside catering.

EPICURE'S LARDER
Middle Wold Farm, Driffield, Wold Newton,
East Yorkshire, YO25 3HY
T: 07769 819 603

Award-winning quality dairy and meat products from the Wolds.

MATTHEWS CHEESE
23-24 Grainger Arcade, Grainger Market, Newcastle
T: 0191 2324265

Continental and English cheese. Over 150 of the finest quality cheeses to choose from. Also a large selection of herbs, spices and a selection of flavoured nuts.

SHEPHERDS PURSE
Leachfield Grange, Newsham,
North Yorkshire, YO7 4DJ
www.shepherdspurse.co.uk
Twitter: @shepherdspurse

Shepherds Purse is a small, family run, artisan cheese company producing the finest, traditional and continental style cheeses on the farm in North Yorkshire.

NORTH ACOMB FARM
Stocksfield, Northumberland, NE43 7UF
T: 01661 843 181

From the finest home produced Aberdeen Angus beef, spring lamb, and outdoor pork, free range poultry and local game to our exclusive range of home prepared pies, cakes and lots more. Everything a farm shop should be.

HODGSON FISH
5 Whitby Street, Hartlepool, TS24 7AD
T: 01429 273 169
www.hodgsonfish.co.uk
Twitter: @hodgsonfish

Established in 1916, Hodgson fish is by far the most experienced wholesaler of fish and seafood in Yorkshire and the North East. Our ethos is simple: supply the freshest sustainable fish to our clients, prepared to the highest specification, without compromise. What makes us special is our unique supply chain, often able to have product from trawler to table within 20 hours, beautifully prepared and packed for the most discerning customers.

BURTREE PUDDINGS
Burtree House, Burtree Lane, Nr Darlington, DL3 0UY
T: 01325 463 521
www.burtreepuddings.co.uk

Home of the sticky toffee pudding! All puddings are made with absolutely the finest ingredients from free range eggs, English butter and of course, their neighbouring organic dairy farm's double cream.

SPURRELLI ICE CREAM
The Old Chandlery, Coquet Street, Amble, NE65 0DJ
T: 01665 710 890
www.spurrelli.com
Twitter: @spurelli

Award-winning boutique ice cream, free wifi, Italian coffee. Ingredients are sourced locally wherever possible, from Virginia's home grown berries to Alnwick Rum.

R.R. FOWLER & SON - BURNHOLME FISHERIES
1 Gerard Avenue, Burnholme, York, YO31 0QT
T: 01904 421 360
fowlersofyork@aol.com

By purchasing fish from markets up and down the east coast of England, and from ports both in the UK and internationally, we are able to bring together all manner of seafood of only the highest quality, to be delivered fresh to your door.

MICHAEL LEE FINE CHEESES
Unit 9 Lister Park, Green Lane Industrial Estate, Featherstone, West Yorkshire, WF7 6FE
www.finecheesesltd.co.uk

Fast growing specialist B2B wholesalers, supplying a vast selection of gourmet cheeses, charcuterie, meat products, tapas and chef's store cupboard items. We buy direct from artisan manufacturers, importing from across the world and maturing cheeses in-house. We offer regular weekly and next day deliveries throughout Yorkshire and further afield. Personal consultation with Michael Lee available upon request. Our extensive experience of retail and wholesale markets keeps us as a leading wholesaler.

NORTHUMBERLAND CHEESE COMPANY
The Cheese Farm, Green Lane, Blagdon, Northumberland, NE13 6BZ
T: 01670 789 798
www.northumberlandcheese.co.uk
Twitter: @NlandCheese

Award-winning Northumberland cheeses made to traditional recipes by a small, hands-on, dedicated team. Established in 1984 by Mark Robertson and based in a small dairy on the Blagdon Estate, we hand-make, wrap and sell a range of 16 cheeses including cow, sheep, goat and Jersey. We may be small, but we have a big passion for handcrafting fine cheese. Every mouthful can be traced back to a single local dairy herd, it's all part of the Northumberland Cheese Company philosophy.

R & J YORKSHIRE'S FINEST FARMERS AND BUTCHERS
Wateredge, Longswales Lane, Kirkby Malzeard, Ripon, North Yorkshire, HG4 3RJ
01765 658611 (24 hours)
01765 658787

Suppliers of the fabulous Waterford Farm Signature Range. The name says it all.

COUNTRY VALLEY FOODS LTD
Hurworth Moor, Darlington, County Durham, DL2 1QH
Leeholme Road, Billingham, TS23 3TA
Darlington T: 01325 720 888
Billingham T: 01642 562 36
www.countryvalley.co.uk

We are the North of England's premier supplier of top quality poultry, beef, lamb, pork, bacon, game and delicatessen products, focusing on traditional and innovative cuisine. We supply and deliver food that matches individual customer specifications in a timely and professional manner.

THE MAGPIES WHITBY CATCH
1 Pier Road, Whitby, North Yorkshire, YO21 3PT
T: 01947 601 313
www.thewhitbycatch.co.uk

The Whitby Catch Online Shop, Whitby's first and only online fish and seafood ordering service! All fish and seafood is prepared to your individual requirement.

HAPPY ORGANIC
Front Street, Cleadon Village, Sunderland, SR6 7PG
T: 0191 5363623 www.happyorganic.org Twitter: @happyorganicNE

Happy Organic features a café and specialist store selling local, organic and natural products. They have a huge range of gluten-free, dairy-free and wheat-free products with all vegetables, eggs, fish and fruit sourced locally. There is also an impressive range of wines, whole foods, organic flours, some homebaked breads, meat from Kielder Organic Meats, free range eggs from Harry Hodgson in County Durham, milk from Acorn Dairy in Darlington, health supplements and now eco-friendly washing products. Company owner, Luisa Minchella, says "Healthy eating has always been close to my heart, with my family involvement in a number of north east food companies, you could say food is in my blood. I used to love visiting places like this down south and I wanted to create a little bit of what I saw and experienced, here in the north east." In the café you can expect sweet treats, including walnut and banana loaf, scones and biscotti to go with your Grumpy Mule coffee or heartier offerings such as Tuscan bean soup, quiche, vegetable and bean curry, homemade pizza and avocado and prawn salad.

It's a family affair

Dad, Romano Minchella, co-owns Bistro Romano, directly opposite Happy Organic on Front Street and also Romano's Italian restaurant in the MetroCentre, with his brother Paolo. Here you will find freshly prepared pasta dishes, steak medallions with a brandy cream sauce, all accompanied with an extensive wine list.

THE BLAGDON FARM SHOP

16-18 Milkhope Centre, Blagdon,
Newcastle upon Tyne, NE13 6DA
T: 01670 789 924
www.theblagdonfarmshop.co.uk
Twitter: @blagdonfarmshop

*Award-winning butcher's shop and traditional
farmhouse kitchen selling Blagdon own produced
beef, pork and poultry, freshly picked produce and
local farm produce.*

OPUS DINING CLUB

Business Park, Pity Me. Durham, DH1 5JZ
T: 0191 388 9926
www.opusdiningclub.co.uk
Twitter: @opusdiningclub

*Gift Baskets - A bespoke gift service for those foodies in
your life. Filled with locally sourced gourmet goodies that
you choose and we deliver. Opus@Home - A personal
shopping service for your dining at home needs. Invite your
guests, choose your menu and we'll deliver all the
ingredients for a fabulous dining experience.*

WWW.TASTECLUBHQ.COM

*TASTECLUB is for lovers of great north food and drink.
Membership is completely free, and provides priority access
to member offers, exclusive collections, gifts and prizes.*

ROUND GREEN DEER FARM – YORKSHIRE VENISON COMPANY

Round Green Lane, Worsbrough,
South Yorkshire, S75 3DR
T: 01226 205 577
info@roundgreenfarm.co.uk
www.roundgreenfarm.co.uk

*Round Green's well-stocked shop not only sells
venison and venison products, but also carries a
range of other game and exotic meats in convenient
packs. They run a wholesale operation that supplies
and delivers portion controlled packs of top quality
venison to the catering trade throughout the UK.
Visit their online store 'Venison for Pets' where
venison bones, sausages, and other venison treats
are now available. Free range eggs, laid on the farm,
are also available.*

SWALLOW FISH LTD

'The Fisherman's Kitchen', 2 South Street,
Seahouses, Northumberland, NE68 7RB
T: 01665 721 052
www.swallowfish.co.uk

*The last fully operational 19th Century smokehouse
in Seahouses, where they smoke kippers, salmon and
fish in the traditional way.*

362
CONTRIBUTORS

Rhian Cradock, The Feathers Inn

Jérôme Cogné, Bouchon Bistrot

NO 59 OLD ELVET
The Durham Marriott Hotel Royal County,
59 Old Elvet, Durham, DH1 3JN
0191 386 6821 (extension 437)
www.DurhamMarriottRoyalCounty.co.uk

THE BAY HORSE HURWORTH
45 The Green, Hurworth, Darlington,
County Durham, DL2 2AA
01325 720 663
www.thebayhorsehurworth.com

BISTRO 21
Aykley Heads House, Aykley Heads,
Durham City, DH1 5AN
0191 384 4354
www.bistrotwentyone.co.uk

THE BLUE BICYCLE
34 Fossgate, York, YO1 9TA
01904 673 990
www.thebluebicycle.com

BOUCHON BISTROT
4-6 Gilesgate, Town Centre,
Hexham, NE46 3NJ
01434 609 943
www.bouchonbistrot.co.uk

THE BRASSERIE
Malmaison Hotel, Quayside,
Newcastle upon Tyne, NE1 3DX
08446 930 658
www.malmaison.com

Christopher Dobson, Café 21

Adam Hegarty, Truffle Restaurant

THE BROAD CHARE
25, Broad Chare, Quayside,
Newcastle upon Tyne, NE1 3DQ
0191 211 2144
www.thebroadchare.co.uk

CAFE 21
Trinity Gardens, Quayside,
Newcastle upon Tyne, NE1 2HH
0191 222 0755
www.cafetwentyone.co.uk

THE CAFE ROYAL
8 Nelson Street,
Newcastle upon Tyne, NE1 5AW
0191 231 3000
www.caferoyalnewcastle.co.uk

CAFFE VIVO
27 Broad Chare, Quayside,
Newcastle upon Tyne, NE1 3DQ
0191 232 1331
www.caffevivo.co.uk

CASTLE EDEN INN
Stockton Road, Castle Eden, Hartlepool,
Cleveland, TS27 4SD
01429 835 137
www.castleedeninn.com

COLMANS
176 - 186 Ocean Road, South Shields,
Tyne and Wear, NE33 2JQ
0191 456 1202
www.colmansfishandchips.com

364 CONTRIBUTORS

David Kennedy at Vallum

Eric Paxman, Eric's

DABBAWAL
69-75 High Bridge,
Newcastle upon Tyne, NE1 6BX
1 Brentwood Mews, Jesmond, NE2 3DG
High Bridge: 0191 232 5133
Jesmond: 0191 281 3434
www.dabbawal.com

DAVID KENNEDY AT VALLUM
Military Road, East Wallhouses,
Newcastle upon Tyne, NE18 0LL
01434 672 406
www.vallumfarm.co.uk

THE DUKE OF WELLINGTON INN
Newton, Nr Corbridge, Northumberland, NE43 7UL
01661 844 446
www.thedukeofwellingtoninn.co.uk

EL GATO NEGRO TAPAS
1 Oldham Road, Ripponden, Sowerby Bridge,
West Yorkshire, HX6 4DN
01422 823 070
www.elgatonegrotapas.com

ERIC'S
73-75 Lidget Street, Lindley, Huddersfield,
West Yorkshire, HD3 3JP
01484 646 416
www.ericsrestaurant.co.uk

Simon Shaw, El Gato Negro Tapas

John Barley, The Wensleydale Heifer

THE FEATHERS INN
Hedley on the Hill, Stocksfield,
Northumberland, NE43 7SW
01661 843 607
www.thefeathers.net

FOURTH FLOOR CAFE & BAR
Harvey Nichols, 107-111 Briggate, Leeds, LS1 6AZ
0113 204 8000
www.harveynichols.com

GRAY'S RESTAURANT AT THE WAREN HOUSE HOTEL
Bamburgh, Northumberland, NE70 7EE
01668 214 581
www.warenhousehotel.co.uk

HEADLAM HALL
Headlam, Near Gainford, Darlington,
County Durham, DL2 3HA
01325 730 238
www.headlamhall.co.uk

THE JOLLY FISHERMAN
Haven Hill, Craster,
Northumberland, NE66 3TR
01665 576 461
www.thejollyfishermancraster.co.uk

LOTUS LOUNGE
Fairfax Court, 32-34 High Street,
Yarm, TS15 9AE
01642 355 558
www.lotus-lounge.co.uk

366
CONTRIBUTORS

Simon Crannage, Samuel's Restaurant

Henny Crosland, The Rose & Crown

THE MAGPIE CAFE
14 Pier Road, Whitby,
North Yorkshire, YO21 3PU
01947 602 058
www.magpiecafe.co.uk

MUSE CONTINENTAL CAFE
104B High Street, Yarm, TS15 9AU
01642 788 558
www.museyarm.com

NINETEEN RESTAURANT
19 Grape Lane, York, YO1 7HU
01904 636 366
www.nineteenyork.com

THE ROSE & CROWN
The Rose & Crown at Romaldkirk,
Barnard Castle,
Co Durham, DL12 9EB
01833 650 213
www.rose-and-crown.co.uk

SAMUEL'S RESTAURANT AND
SWINTON PARK COOKERY SCHOOL
Swinton Park, Masham, Ripon,
North Yorkshire, HG4 4JH
Samuel's: 01765 680 900
Cookery School: 01765 680 969
www.swintonpark.com

James Martin and Craig Atchinson, The Talbot Hotel

Matthew Barker, The Westwood Restaurant

SHIBDEN MILL INN
Shibden Mill Fold, Shibden, Halifax,
West Yorkshire, HX3 7UL
01422 365 840
www.shibdenmillinn.com

THE TALBOT HOTEL
Yorkersgate, Malton, North Yorkshire, YO17 7AJ
01653 639 096
www.talbotmalton.co.uk

TRUFFLE RESTAURANT
20 Grange Road, Darlington,
County Durham, DL1 5NG
01325 483 787
www.trufflerestaurant.co.uk

THE WENSLEYDALE HEIFER
Main St, West Witton, Yorkshire, DL8 4LS
01969 622 322
www.wensleydaleheifer.co.uk

WENTBRIDGE HOUSE
Wentbridge House Hotel, The Great North Road,
Wentbridge, Pontefract, West Yorkshire, WF8 3JJ
01977 620 444
www.wentbridgehouse.co.uk

THE WESTWOOD RESTAURANT
New Walk, Beverley, East Yorkshire, HU17 7AE
01482 881 999
www.thewestwood.co.uk

BEST OF BRITISH

Relish Publications is an independent publishing house offering an exclusive insight into Britain's finest restaurants and chefs through their series of award-winning recipe books.

Each book contains signature recipes from your favourite chefs, recommended wines, stunning food photography and an impressive guide to each participating restaurant, plus a larder featuring the region's best produce suppliers. These ingredients make the Relish series an ultimate 'foodies' guide for individuals wishing to dine in great restaurants or create outstanding recipes at home.

The series of beautiful hard back recipe books are available to buy in the featured restaurants, all good bookshops and online at the Relish bookshop or on Amazon.

For more information please visit **www.relishpublications.co.uk**

RelishDIGITAL

LOOKING TO DINE IN THE UK'S FINEST RESTAURANTS?

Visit the Relish Restaurant Guide to find the very best your region has to offer.

The Relish team has worked with all of the chefs listed on the Relish website and have visited every highly recommended and acclaimed restaurant. This recipe makes the **Relish Restaurant Guide** genuine and unique.

If you would like to be taken on an epic journey to the finest restaurants in each region, to download more mouth-watering recipes, to join our exclusive Relish Rewards club, or to add to your collection of Relish books, visit **www.relishpublications.co.uk**

WHAT'S APP-ENING?

All of our regional cookbooks are now available to download and purchase.

Browse hundreds of recipes with beautiful photography and easy to follow instructions from a selection of the UK's finest chefs and restaurants.

 Download your FREE sample pages now on the App Store/Relish Cookbook.

Apple, the Apple logo and iPhone are trademarks of Apple Inc, registered in the US and other countries, App Store is a service mark of Apple Inc.

Relish PUBLICATIONS

Duncan and Teresa Peters founded Relish Publications in 2009, through a passion for good food, a love of publishing and after recognising the need to promote the fantastic chefs and restaurants each region in the UK has to offer.

Since launching, their goal was simple. Create beautiful books with high quality contributors (each edition features a selection of the region's top chefs) to build a unique and invaluable recipe book.

As recipe book specialists, their team work with hundreds of chefs personally to ensure each edition exceeds the readers' expectations.

Thank you for Relishing with us!

HERE'S WHAT SOME OF BRITAIN'S BEST CHEFS HAVE SAID ABOUT WORKING WITH RELISH

"The Relish cookbook offers the home cook some great inspiration to make the most of these wonderful ingredients in season." *Tom Kitchin, The Kitchin, Edinburgh*

"Relish Publications are always very impressive books, beautifully assembled, with fabulous images and a real pleasure to absorb." *Geoffrey Smeddle, The Peat Inn, St Andrews*

"Relish Wales is a fabulous way to showcase some of our beautiful country's fabulous eateries and to be able to share our food with a wider audience." *Stephen Terry, The Hardwick, Wales*

"I'm immensely proud to be writing the foreword to a book that celebrates the best of Midland's food." *Andreas Antona, Simpsons Restaurant, Birmingham*

371 GLOSSARY

BAIN-MARIE
A pan or other container of hot water with a bowl placed on top of it. This allows the steam from the water to heat the bowl so ingredients can be gently heated or melted in the bowl.

BALLOTINE
A traditional ballotine is a deboned leg of a chicken, duck or other poultry stuffed with ground meat and other ingredients, tied and cooked, usually by braising or poaching. A modern ballotine can be made using any type of meat, and served hot or cold.

BLANCH
Boiling an ingredient before removing it and plunging it in ice cold water in order to stop the cooking process.

BLIND BAKE
Partially or completely baking a pastry base before adding the filling, to create a stronger crust that can hold moist filling without getting soggy. Useful also when a filling needs less time to cook than the pastry.

BLOOM (GELATINE)
Blooming gelatine is the process of soaking it in water to make sure it dissolves evenly. Gelatine is placed in a bowl of cold water and left to soak for a few minutes, before being added to a mixture.

BOUDIN
Boudin is the name of a French sausage, but is also used to describe food prepared in a sausage-like shape.

BRUNOISE
A culinary knife cut in which the food item is first julienned and then turned 90 degrees and diced again, producing cubes of about 3mm or less on each side.

CHINOIS
A conical sieve with an extremely fine mesh. It is used to strain custards, purées, soups and sauces, producing a very smooth texture.

CLARIFIED BUTTER
Milk fat rendered from butter to separate the milk solids and water from the butter fat.

CONFIT
A method of cooking where the meat is cooked and submerged in a liquid to add flavour. Often this liquid is rendered fat. Confit can also apply to fruits - fruit confits are cooked and preserved in sugar, the result is like candied fruits.

CREPINETTE
Crépine is the French word for 'pig's caul' in which a crépinette is wrapped instead of a casing.

EMULSION/EMULSIFY
In the culinary arts, an emulsion is a mixture of two liquids that would ordinarily not mix together, like oil and vinegar.

JULIENNE
A culinary knife cut in which the food item is cut into long thin strips, similar to matchsticks.

PANE
To coat with flour, beaten egg and breadcrumbs.

QUENELLE
An elegant way of presenting purées, ice-creams, mousses or anything of similar consistency by moulding into neat oval shapes using two spoons.

SABAYON
Made by beating egg yolks with a liquid over simmering water until thickened and increased in volume. The liquid can be water, but Champagne or wine is often used.

SHUCK/SHUCKED (OYSTERS)
Removal of oysters from their shells.

TEMPER (CHOCOLATE)
'Tempering is like organising individuals dancers at a party into a Conga line. For chocolate, temperature and motion are the party organisers that bring all the individual dancing crystals of fatty acids together in long lines and, in the process, create a stable crystallisation throughout the chocolate mass.' Chocomap.com

TURNED
Turning vegetables means to pare down vegetables into even, identical shapes, usually ovals with seven sides